title

Windows 11 User Guide: 2021-2022 Complete Windows 11 User Guide. 55 Best Features and Tips Included

title

Copyright © 2021

All rights reserved.

ISBN:

title

© **Copyright 2021 - All rights reserved.**

The content contained within this book may not be reproduced, duplicated or transmitted without direct written permission from the author or the publisher.

Under no circumstances will any blame or legal responsibility be held against the publisher, or author, for any damages, reparation, or monetary loss due to the information contained within this book. Either directly or indirectly. You are responsible for your own choices, actions, and results.

Legal Notice:

This book is copyright protected. This book is only for personal use. You cannot amend, distribute, sell, use, quote or paraphrase any part, or the content within this book, without the consent of the author or publisher.

Disclaimer Notice:

Please note the information contained within this document is for educational and entertainment purposes only. All effort has been

title

executed to present accurate, up-to-date, and reliable, complete information. No warranties of any kind are declared or implied. Readers acknowledge that the author is not engaging in the rendering of legal, financial, medical, or professional advice. The content within this book has been derived from various sources. Please consult a licensed professional before attempting any techniques outlined in this book.

title

CONTENTS

Introduction — 8
    Initial Thoughts on Windows 11 — 9
    What Are the Benefits of Computer Training for Seniors? — 14
    What PC Skills Do Seniors Need to Know? — 16
    How Can Seniors Learn Basic PC Skills? — 17
    Seniors Learning How to Use PCs Need… — 19
    What is Windows 11? — 25

Chapter 1: How to install Windows 11? — 28
    Make Sure Your Laptop or Computer Is Supported — 29
    Installing Software or Applications on Windows Isn't Working? Here's What You Should Do — 38
    Three Ways of Installing Windows 11 on Computers That Are Not Supported — 53

Chapter 2: What is Interface? — 66
    User Interfaces Types — 67

Chapter 3: What are Web Browsers? — 94
    Examples of Web Browsers — 95
    Browser Slowness in Windows 11 Troubleshooting — 98
    Applications and Services in the Background Should be Turned off or Killed — 101

Chapter 4: What are the Benefits of Windows 11? — 115
    What's the Huge Deal with Windows 11? — 115
    Windows 11's Seven Most Valuable Features — 117
    How to Turn Off/On Windows 11 Notifications — 120
    Hotkeys: What Are They and How Do You Use Them? — 126
    How to Connect to a Network in Windows 11 — 128

When Your Windows 11 PC Cannot Establish a Connection, What Should You Do?   132

Chapter 5: How to Adjust Display Scale Settings in Windows 11   140

How to Adjust the Display Size in Windows 11 Using Custom Settings? 141

Windows 11: A Partially Complete, Lent Heritage from Windows 10X 148

Conclusion   173

Introduction

For several seniors out there, using a PC is a novel experience, and the prospect of discovering and participating in the online realm may be fascinating. A PC may help seniors communicate with relatives via electronic mail and videoconferencing, keep their brains busy by gaming and acquiring new skills, and even form new, healthful relationships by allowing them to communicate with individuals who are engaged in similar activities with them.

A computer, on the other hand, might be daunting and intimidating to individuals who've never made use of one prior. Conventional UIs are hard to use, symbols and graphics are tiny and hard to see, and appropriate help is frequently unavailable. Some digital newbies may be scared off by tales of viruses, malware, and breakdowns, and some may be afraid that they could "damage" their PC by accidentally clicking or pressing the wrong key or symbol. Hence, having easy access to continuing technical help is crucial in easing the newcomer's transition to digital technology.

Initial Thoughts on Windows 11

Although some modifications might take some becoming accustomed to, Windows 11 features several good interface enhancements that help productivity in this initial build.

Windows 11 is now in its early version, and it is still far from fully complete; during this stage of the rollout, the emphasis is usually on ensuring app and hardware compliance. Since they didn't have their 2.0 TPMs (Trusted Platform Modules) switched on (a straightforward repair) or Secure Boot activated, some computers out there won't effectively use Windows 11.

However, you can properly install Windows 11 beta on your machine if only you can follow a few recommended steps that would be outlined in the later parts of this book. If you want to attempt installing Windows 11 on your PC, we recommend that you do so overnight because the update takes a long time. Below is our first impression of the new Microsoft operating system.

The User Interface

The taskbar in Windows 11 resembles a hybrid of what you'll see in the taskbar of Windows 10 and macOS dock, with the only difference being that there are no animations. It justifies the icons by moving them to the taskbar's center instead of the left. The revamped Start menu in this new operating system is centrally placed, and instead of a list, it displays applications in the form of a grid.

In fact, accessing the program index is identical, but the end effect is significantly distinct and much similar to what you'd see on your smartphone: your most frequently used applications are sorted alphabetically rather than a list, as they were in previous editions of Windows. This modification will render it much easier for you to locate certain programs than it would have been previously.

Changing to the full application list is simple and fast, but it's only a step above the standard application list that was featured previously. The overall impression is similar to what we're accustomed to on smartphones, like with the standard application list. It does appear more practical as soon you've gotten acclimated to the latest layout.

When you click the Windows symbol that still maintains its left-hand position, only that it is now centrally placed with some other application symbols in your PC's taskbar, settings do not appear right away. The home screen symbols and backdrop remains untouched. right When you enter Settings, though, the design is drastically changed, and it might take some time to figure out where the right setting you'd like has been relocated.

The coronavirus outbreak brought in a new approach to work, and things might never revert back to how they used to be, even as people begin to return to their jobs. In Windows 11, the interface of the Settings application has changed dramatically.

However, the options that you most frequently use will be visible rather than hidden behind a submenu, saving you ample time that you can channel to other activities. As soon as you've gotten acclimated to the latest Settings design, you'll probably see that it is more effective to utilize than the application listings.

Integration With Smartphones

This early iteration is being worked on by Microsoft's smartphone interoperability program, Your Phone, which does a good job of presenting an onscreen display of a few of your device's basic functionality including phone calls and SMS. It looks to have music functionality too, although it seems to be deactivated at the moment. Some Windows fans will like how they could move an image from their smartphone's visual representation to their system desktop interface and send it. The software is now both easily usable and more helpful than it was before.

Performance

The new operating system is often not optimized for great performance at this stage of the deployment. On some Dell computers, though, we did not see any particular wait conditions or speed reduction. This absence of apparent performance cost implies that, as we come nearer to the OS's formal launch, there could be a minor performance improvement.

There are some really great enhancements with this new rollout of Windows. Although, it is not particularly impressive. But, that's to be anticipated, when the focus is mostly on software/hardware compliance and the product doesn't yet feature comprehensively. This stage of the evaluation isn't intended to be overly interesting; it's just obliged to perform, and the new operating system did so with little retraining.

Google Cloud's environment can be of help in streamlining your data management, distributing data access, and assisting provide outstanding business results.

The latest operating system is great by most standards with no real issues. At least, essential applications will function correctly, and Your Phone app will show a usability increase, even if one of the newest features didn't seem to be operational yet. Your Phone is a convenient way of seeing alerts, texts, phone calls, and images on your smartphone.

Anyone running Windows 11 on a three-year-old business desktop, laptop, or PC with Secure Boot and TPM 2.0 will encounter something similar. If your computer doesn't have a contemporary TPM, it might not be able to install Windows 11.

Because a lot of computers support Secure Boot and TPM 2.0 but aren't enabled, the Secure Boot and TPM 2.0 specifications for your Windows 11 system ought to lead to far more protections. Other frameworks will have to be supplanted, albeit not immediately: support for Windows 10 will be available until the year 2025.

With the rise in ransomware and other forms of cyberattacks, it is indeed a wise thing to consider upgrading to the current Windows edition sooner instead of later. Nevertheless, it's better to wait for some time after the general debut before implementing to ensure that any new issues are discovered and fixed before proceeding. In holiday seasons, this type of update is often a great idea because any issues wouldn't have a toll on your overall productivity.

Last but not least, after installing Windows 11, the security features are normally turned off. This means that you have to manually turn them on. If you install the latest edition of Windows 11, make sure to check these functionalities; the absurdity of implementing a more secure edition of Windows 11 just to discover that security is disabled is excruciating at best.

What Are the Benefits of Computer Training for Seniors?

All things computerized have a paralyzing terror in the minds of older individuals. Unlike today's youngsters, they presumably only had a TV to handle during their childhoods. It's only normal for them if they are sentimental and avoid technology. However, if you're reading this, you already know how important it is to master fundamental computer skills. Use these three arguments to persuade your parents or older relatives on why they should learn how to use one:

To Handle Day-to-Day Needs

Digitization is gradually infiltrating our daily lives. Electronic repositories now house our health records. Online banking services have moved our money to the internet as well. Some activities are now far more straightforward to conduct online than offline. For a time, we can dodge these adjustments, but never forever. Take a peek around today's shops. There are fewer retail workers and more automated kiosks, albeit not all of the latter can handle cash. It is important that seniors learn to work with these screens regularly. With the widespread use of smartphones and the growth of banking applications such as PayLah and PayNow, this might not be long before cash is phased out.

For Entertainment

If they struggle to admit they have "no option," attempt to persuade them that it is indeed a "good decision." As your folks get older, they're more likely to be working less and spend more time doing things they enjoy. Consider this: What do they enjoy doing? Do you enjoy Taiwanese dramas? Do you like listening to music from the 1970s? Do you like to read books on world politics? Whatever their hobbies, there are sure to be a plethora of applications that may immediately enhance the qualities of their living.

To Strengthen Family Ties

Older individuals are prone to want intergenerational connection in addition to entertainment. Asking for your assistance could be your older folks' method of expressing their worry! Learning fundamental PC and smartphone skills, on the other hand, will only help your parents to have more regular and good contact. Knowing how to use social media platforms is one of the most beneficial for this reason. Seventy-seven percent of Singaporeans have access to social media platforms. Instagram isn't only for the youngsters; thirty-three percent of web users are aged between fifty-five and sixty-five. Seniors who can traverse these platforms alone will be far better able to keep up with what their kids and grandkids are doing, even if they're staying in the same house.

What PC Skills Do Seniors Need to Know?

It's one thing to persuade seniors to learn basic PC skills, and it is a completely different thing to get them to actually use it in your absence. Furthermore, what competencies should they acquire? Where should they begin?

To assist you, we've compiled a non-exhaustive compendium of important abilities that are particularly useful to older citizens. Learning basic computer skills helps elders overcome their phobia of technology, allowing them to use computers in their daily lives. After learning the fundamentals, seniors can go to learn introductory skills that will help them navigate the virtual world more safely and comfortably.

Computer Fundamentals

- Understanding of computer components such as the USB port, mouse, camera, and earphone jack
- Self-assurance when using computers and mobile devices
- Creating, saving, and deleting files and programs

- Use of the internet for basic purposes
- Signing in, receiving, and responding to emails (fundamental email operations)
- Spreadsheet and document creation, printing, and saving.

Fundamental PC Skills

- Becoming familiar with storage concepts such as files, directories, and compression
- Fundamental network concepts such as connectivity, uploading, and downloading are well-understood.
- Being aware of security threats such as file security, malware, and internet security
- Changing the settings on mobile devices and computers
- Utilization of social media platforms such as Instagram and Facebook
- Utilization of interactive web tools such as video conferencing, instant messaging, and online diaries
- Synchronization and storage in the cloud

How Can Seniors Learn Basic PC Skills?

Some of these tasks may appear to us to be straightforward and obvious, but they could be completely unfamiliar to seniors. Below are five suggestions for assisting older persons in effectively learning new PC skills:

Stay Away from Jargon

The more information you have, the less probable you are to be understood. This implies you'll have to try a bit harder to translate your expertise into an easy, common language if you want to be comprehended by computer newbies.

Adapt to Their Likes and Dislikes

Actively attempt to attract their attention by appealing to their preferences, in addition to avoiding destroying their enthusiasm with nonsensical phrases. If we utilize our creativity, learning PC and mobile abilities can be fun!

Familiarize Yourself by Touching

Allowing older individuals to engage with electronics without constraint can help them cope with some psychological hurdles. Allow them to touch the connections, type nonsense, and tap the desktop screens. Laugh along with them, and *boom* - their dread will go.

Practice Patience

It is important that you don't become irritated or pass judgment on your seniors when they mess up. Allow them to take pauses and congratulate them when it is obvious to them that they made some progress. Make yourself a copy of your top teachers and try out different things to see what feels right for them.

Rehearse, Rehearse, Rehearse

Lastly, if seniors do not continue to improve their computer abilities, all of the personalized advice will be for naught. Repetition could be tedious, therefore relying on expert training will be really beneficial. The involvement of contemporaries at comparable phases of learning can encourage older folks in ways that you would not be able to do on your own.

Seniors Learning How to Use PCs Need…

Encouragement

Many older citizens desire to learn about using PCs, but they're unsure about their own abilities. Providing them with efficient technical support can help alleviate these concerns. For seniors who are just laying their hands on a PC for the first time, anxieties that are peculiar to learning new skills as a first-timer. If you are just starting out with PCs as a senior, you want to consult a younger person with a lot of tech experience to guide you through and encourage you. It is not uncommon to find yourself asking some of the most ridiculous questions as a senior PC user who isn't very conversant with tech. Your much younger PC guide should be patient enough to answer your queries in the easiest possible way.

Incremental Steps

Also, some of the most adept PC users understand how to teach new abilities in small increments. A lot of seniors have never worked with a pc before. Your PC guide will teach you how to operate the cursor, left and right-click on the mouse, and type using the keyboard. Then you'll learn more applicable things like sending emails and engaging in a teleconferencing session since that is one of the most crucial uses of PCs for seniors as they'll always like to get in touch with their family members. Also, most seniors would like to learn how to browse so they can surf their favorite news sites and check out the latest happenings around the globe. To avoid feeling overwhelmed with many things to learn, you want to learn one thing at a time. This will help you acquire the much-needed confidence in forging ahead.

"Language" Barrier

Unawareness of computer lingo is another impediment for some elderly attempting to use one. Beginner PC users are unlikely to grasp instructions using phrases like "URL search bar" or "search bar" if they have never heard them before. If you feel lost, consult an adept computer user who understands the need of explaining ideas and commands in a way that is understandable. This is also why having remote access is such a valuable advantage for system users.

The reassurance that comes with the knowledge that they can request the assistance of a patient and a kind individual to answer a query is a big motivation for seniors who'd like to learn how to use a computer. Technical support can help users overcome their anxieties and doubts about their capacity to learn crucial computer skills.

Technology Encourages Elderly to Live Independently

Poor treatment compliance and safety issues owing to diminished mobility are two major factors that render independent living challenging for some seniors. As a result, their safety and health could be jeopardized. New technology, on the other hand, is poised to resist this.

Indeed, the advent of computers has had a remarkable impact on the medical world. Patients can now receive a message on their phone reminding them when to take their prescription.

Caregivers can now be notified if their clients fail to affirm that they have taken their medications. Several more health-related devices and applications have been created in recent years.

Prescription reminders, a pulse monitoring gadget, and even applications that can instantly arrange for a medication refill are all tools that help older folks manage and monitor their health. Modern health devices, like accident detection devices and smart wearables, are also available for seniors to try out.

They have a medicine reminder crown that lights when it is time to take their prescription, and also step counting and a call-for-help, single-push button. Furthermore, smart equipment that could be shut off automatically, like home cleaning machines, makes living independently comfier and easier for the elderly. Certainly, technology gives seniors the security they need to be self-sufficient. This gives their relatives the assurance that they can help their parents avoid relocating to an eldercare facility.

Technology Allows Family Members and Friends to Stay in Touch With One Another

Because of today's technology, interaction has never been simpler. It's primarily because of the world wide web! Using instant messengers, deliver texts right away. Freely call and view relatives and friends (no matter where they are) using FaceTime or Skype. Use social media platforms like Facebook and Twitter to reconnect with long-lost relatives and friends. In real-time, users may send videos and photos of their family members. Technology is undeniably important in overcoming communication gaps, maintaining family relationships, and building bonds.

Staying in contact is among the most intriguing elements of modern technology, whether you use a mobile phone, an iPad, or a laptop.

Technology Maintains Your Interest and Keeps People Interested

The modern-day playground and theater are the world wide web. On your PC, you may watch movies. Netflix opens you up to their entire video collection if you sign up for a subscription. They offer tens of thousands of films and TV episodes to choose from. iTunes, Hulu, and Amazon Instant Video are a few other TV show and movie subscription services.

Computer Games Abound on the Web

For example, the AARP internet games are created to help seniors improve their cognitive and memory abilities.

Video game consoles, on the other hand, have progressed significantly. Wii and Xbox Kinect are two examples of video game systems that can get you moving. They're not just a fun way to pass the time, but they're also a fantastic way to get some exercise. Sony's PlayStation and Microsoft's Xbox are two other gaming consoles. Seniors can benefit greatly from these entertainment devices, even more than the youngsters do.

Technology Aids in The Communication of Elderly Persons

Seniors can keep up with what's going on in the United States and across the globe. Online news sites can provide you with up-to-date information.

Technology allows seniors to work more efficiently

Numerous productivity applications are available to assist seniors in remaining ordered and efficient. Evernote, for example, is a tool that can increase senior's productivity and it also doubles as a filing system. Because it arranges it all for you, it serves to keep distractions at bay. Countless seniors are uninitiated in terms of technology, the world wide web, applications, and other devices. It is possible to learn almost anything. Indeed, some websites assist seniors in learning basic computer and internet skills. For instance, SeniorNet provides computer training and assistance with technological devices and internet-related issues. Also, seniors can keep schooling by enrolling in e-learning ranging from design and architecture to web design and engineering, all of which can be completed from the comfort of their own homes.

Technology Isn't Here to Destroy or Jeopardize Our Lives

In fact, the situation is the inverse. Technology can assist us in becoming more knowledgeable so that we can gain valuable insights into the world around us. It is crucial for seniors to accept it. It's simple and enjoyable to embrace technology. Begin!

What is Windows 11?

Windows 11 is Windows 10's successor, which debuted sometime in 2015, and is the latest upgrade of the Windows operating system created by Microsoft. It was launched on 24th June 2021.

On 5th October 2021, Windows 11 was made available to the general public as a non-paid software upgrade for qualified Windows 10 gadgets through the use of Installation Assistant for Windows 11 and Windows Update.

Windows 11 includes a revamped Start menu, the substitute of the "live tiles" plus a different "Widgets" tab on its taskbar, the capacity to customize tiled collections of screens that you can restore and minimize from your system taskbar as a cluster, and latest gaming innovations handed down from the Xbox Series S and Series X like DirectStorage and Auto HDR on compliant hardware. The standard browser has now been supplanted with the Chromium-centered Microsoft Edge, while Microsoft Teams has now been incorporated in the Windows desktop. Microsoft revealed plans to provide applications sold through the Microsoft Store greater freedom, as well as enable Android applications on the new operating system (plus cooperation with Amazon marketplace to render its application store accessible for the role).

The system specs for Windows 11 have been raised above Windows 10 due to security concerns. Only gadgets with an 8th-gen Intel Processor or later, AMD Ryzen Processor centered on the Zen+ microarchitecture or later, or Qualcomm Snapdragon 850 or later, with Trusted Platform Module 2.0 and UEFI secure boot support and activated, are fully supported by Microsoft. While the operating system could be installed on CPUs that aren't supported, Microsoft cannot promise that updates will be available. Also, Windows 11 removes compatibility for x86 32-bit processors and BIOS-based gadgets.

Pre-launch coverage of Windows 11 centered on the OS's tighter hardware specifications, with debates over if they were truly meant to increase Windows security or merely a gimmick to upsell customers to newer gadgets, as well as concerns regarding e-waste related to the modifications. When it was first released, Windows 11 was praised for its enhanced design aesthetic, window organization, and safety emphasis, but it was derided for regressions and changes to the UI.

Chapter 1: How to install Windows 11?

Windows 11 is now ready for download on all compatible systems, and you don't have to wait for the free upgrade to arrive.

Windows 11 is currently available. Microsoft officially introduced its new OS on 5th October but cautioned that most consumers will have to wait a long time to transition from Windows 10 for free. If you are using outdated gadgets that are still compatible, the upgrade might not arrive until mid-2022.

There is no point waiting that long, though. The new operating system is now downloadable as an ISO file directly from the Microsoft official website, as well as an almost-ultimate edition through the Windows Insider Program. Both techniques are absolutely free and shouldn't take more than a couple of minutes to finish.

Before we go any further, let's define what we meant by 'ultimate edition.' This includes any edition issued after October 5th; however, Windows 11 will keep getting upgrades for the rest of its lifecycle. That's normally one decade; for example, Windows 10 was introduced in 2015, but it'll receive upgrades until 2025.

That's not, however, the simplest approach to switch to Windows 11. Microsoft is progressively pushing out the patch to all eligible devices over the months ahead, but the corporation has stated that it is "moving up the rate of the deployment quicker than it originally planned." Before proceeding with the methods in this section, check to see if it has landed on your gadget under Settings.

Make Sure Your Laptop or Computer Is Supported

If you've not previously done so, double-check that your Windows 10 gadget is compliant with Windows 11. The giant tech company has revised the system requirements, which means that a lot of older technology will no longer be enabled.

The simplest method of finding out would be to download Microsoft's new PC Health Check program, which is freely available and requires only a few minutes to set up. While you may have to physically activate Secure Boot or TPM 2.0, and both are essential, it's far more dependable than the initial generation.

Even on incompatible systems, though, a hack allows you to install Windows 11. After you've handled it, you may move on to the installation process.

Here's How to Obtain Windows 11 Right Now: Get the ISO File

Right now, the quickest method to acquire Windows 11 is to get this via Microsoft's official website. There are two alternatives available, both will preserve all of your settings and data.

The 'Windows 11 Installation Assistant,' which will walk you through the procedure, is recommended for most individuals, especially seniors. But the gadget you use to access it has to have the following features:

- A Microsoft Windows 10 license (if the operating system was already pre-installed when you acquired the gadget, it'll come with one)
- You're using 2004 edition or higher (May 2020 upgrade)
- A minimum of nine gigabytes of hard drive space
- If it satisfies all of these requirements, you may begin the installation process:
- Click 'Download Now' in the 'Windows 11 Installation Assistant' section
- A tiny.exe file will be automatically downloaded to your computer. To open it, double-click it.
- Select 'Yes' to indicate that you agree to the modifications.

If you want to have Windows 11 installed on several computers, you need to get the ISO file rather. It's a considerably bigger package, but it has everything you need to have Windows 11 installed.

Simply ensure you've got a minimum of eight gigabytes of storage space available anywhere you send it, along with a reliable external storage unit. Every computer you deploy it on should also fulfill Windows 11's system specifications, including a 64-bit processor and a language that mirrors your existing one.

Getting Windows 11: Through the Insider Program

The Insider Program was the only option to get a head start on Windows 11 before this was announced. Within the Release Preview Channel, you may get an almost-ultimate edition.

If you've not already done that, you ought to join the Windows Insider Program for this approach. Go to the Microsoft website's landing page and select 'Register,' then take the procedures to link your Microsoft account.

Following that, below is what you'll have to do from your Windows 10 gadget:

- A pop-up screen will show, guiding you step-by-step via the procedure.

- Select 'Windows Insider Program' from the left-hand panel of Settings > Update & Security.

- Select 'Get started' then sign in with the same Microsoft account that you utilized to sign up in the Insider Program.

- Complete the on-screen instructions, ensuring that you pick the 'Release Preview Channel' option.

- Accept the terms of service, then restart your computer to affect the settings when requested.

- Go to Settings > Update & Security when you've gotten everything fully backed up and operational. You ought to see the choice to download Windows 11 if you have installed all prior patches.

- To start the upgrading procedure, select 'Download and install.' Because your gadget would be out of operation for a long time, ensure you plan beforehand.

If you've already implemented an early release of Windows 11, all you have to do now is update the Insider Program path:

- Go to Settings > Windows Update.

- Select 'Windows Insider Program' from the 'More choices' menu.

- Choose 'Release Preview Channel' from the 'Choose Insider options' menu.

- Return to the Windows Update home page and select 'Check for updates.'

- It may take a couple of minutes for this process to complete, but you'll ultimately notice an upgrade will become accessible. If you're reading this, you're already using the most recent version.

Choose 'Stop obtaining preview updates' from the same Windows Insider Program options bar if you'd not like access to initial builds in times ahead. If you don't select 'Unenroll this computer when the upcoming Windows edition is released,' you will need to reinstall Windows 10.

Installing Windows 11 Using a USB Drive

Microsoft has formally announced that ISO files for its Windows 11 are now available, allowing users to run it from their USB drives or other flash devices. Below is how it works:

Although Windows 11 was first introduced in June, it is now available for free download. Currently, there are a few new gadgets with the operating system pre-installed, and there will be lots more shortly.

You may install Windows 11 right now if you've got a suitable Windows 10 computer. The download page of Windows 11 is now available, and the Installation Assistant makes getting started a breeze.

You'll also see the official Microsoft ISO file there. It's the quickest and most convenient method to copy it into a USB drive or other memory card and run it on as many compatible gadgets as you want.

Despite Microsoft's official backing, the procedure is still fairly difficult. Below is all you have to know about it.

Make sure you have adequate room for installation

Before you start, double-check that you will not exhaust your installation room at any point. Because the ISO file of Windows is about 5.1GB, you need enough space on the computer where it's installed, as well as any memory sticks you're utilizing and the targeted gadgets.

If it's getting difficult, our advice to clearing up storage in your Windows 10-powered system may be of assistance. It's advisable to back up any files you won't need right away and then conduct a system restore. You may then pick what you like when you go back to your computer.

Get the ISO File

Logging into your Microsoft account and enrolling for Microsoft's Windows Insider Program were previously required steps in the download procedure. It's a lot easier now:

- Go to the download page of Windows 11 on the Microsoft website.
- Select 'Download Now' in the 'Create Windows 11 installation media' option
- The Creation Tool should start downloading at this point. Double-click it as soon as it's completed to execute it.
- Get the ISO file by following the step-by-step instructions.

Ensure you choose this selection if you have to preserve any of your current files or data. After the installation, Windows 11 should operate as if the gadget had just been unboxed. But, installing it using a USB drive is a little more difficult.

- Copy it to your USB drive.

The first step is straightforward. Like just about other download files, the ISO file should show in your system's File Explorer (If you are using a Mac, it should show in the Finder section). Simply connect your USB drive or other memory stick to your computer and upload the file as usual — it's a large file, hence this might require one or two minutes.

- Ensure you remove it before disconnecting it after it's on your USB.

Starting Windows 11 from Your USB Drive

This is when things start to get complicated. If you want to utilize that USB drive to execute Windows 11 after it's connected, you'll have to make it bootable.

Rufus is recommended by Microsoft for this process:

- Download and install the most recent edition of Rufus on the gadget that also features Windows 11.

- Connect the USB drive that will be used to deploy the ISO file. Ascertain that it has a minimum of eight gigabytes of free space and that all other items have been deleted.

- Select the required USB within 'Device' from the primary Rufus panel.

- Within 'File system,' choose NTFS, and within 'Partition scheme,' choose MBR.

- Choose 'SELECT' adjacent to 'Boot selection' then select the ISO file.

- To start the procedure, select 'Start'; the time it takes is contingent on how fast your USB drive is.

- After you've finished, you'll get a USB drive that you can utilize to install Windows 11 on just about any enabled device.

- Insert the USB flash drive into the desired gadget.

- Reboot your computer.

- Press the F8 key before the famous Windows logo displays to activate Safe Mode.

- Choose 'Use a device' as well as the USB drive from the menu.

The ISO file of Windows 11 that you got must now boot up on your computer. If this is not the case, you might have to disable Secure Boot within the BIOS configuration.

Installing Software or Applications on Windows Isn't Working? Here's What You Should Do

Why are you unable to install any applications on your Windows 11-powered PC? When software installations refuse to run, produce an error message, or appear to operate normally but ultimately fail, it's irritating.

When programs won't install on your Windows 11 computer, then it is time to try out the solutions listed below.

Restart Your PC

This is a standard troubleshooting procedure, but it's crucial for a purpose. It's possible that the reason the software isn't running on your PC is due to a momentary issue. You should restart to return to a pristine condition before moving on to more targeted solutions.

Keep troubleshooting with the following procedure if you are still finding it hard to install applications after a restart.

In Windows, Look for The App Installer Settings

Both standard desktop software and applications from Microsoft Store may be installed on Windows 11. You should first check your settings to see if they limit you to just implementing Store applications.

Go to Settings > Apps > Apps & Features to do so. Deciding where to obtain applications is located in the upper part of the page. You cannot install programs from elsewhere if the selection is adjusted to Microsoft Store alone (recommended). You won't be able to install typical Windows desktop apps because of this.

Modify these settings to Anywhere and Windows will no longer prevent you from installing applications.

If you are using an earlier version of Windows 10, go to Settings > Update & Security > For developers and look for a setting that is similar. Ensure that Sideload applications are chosen in the Use developer features section. You may be unable to run ordinary software if you choose Microsoft Store programs.

These three choices are not available in recent editions of Windows 11. Rather, you'll get a single slider for Developer Mode. Because you don't need this to run programs on Windows 11, you can turn it off. It's not a bad idea to activate it while debugging, but if everything is functioning, you may like to have it turned off.

Lastly, you can only run programs from Microsoft Store if you are using Windows 11. Fortunately, switching out of Windows 11 is simple and free.

Increase Storage Space on The Hard drive

You might find it hard to install new applications if you are running out of storage space. Although this is seldom an issue with tiny programs, downloading large-scale software like Adobe products or Microsoft Office can take multiple gigabytes.

Execute the Installer with Administrative Privileges

UAC (User Account Control) in Windows ensures that your Microsoft account only utilizes its administrative rights when absolutely essential. When you attempt installing a new application, you'll normally get a UAC popup because most software needs admin credentials to install.

It's possible that you won't require administrator access if you are merely deploying an application for your logged-in Microsoft account. Installing programs that affect all users, on the other hand, will need admin clearance. If you've got UAC switched off, requests to provide administrator permissions may not display.

Authorizing a UAC inquiry may not always operate properly. You may receive an error message stating that the app installer is unable to access a specific folder, or that the app installer may fail to execute whatsoever. You should execute the installation as an administrator in these circumstances.

If the installation window is active, shut it first, then proceed to right-clicking on the app installer file and select Run as admin. Try the installation again after providing admin permissions to see whether it works.

Ask anyone good with computers if you do not have admin privileges on your present system to help you out when you may feel lost.

Verify that the Application is 64-bit Compatible

Many programs are available in both the 64-bit and 32-bit versions. Only 64-bit Windows versions are interoperable with 64-bit apps. However, because 64-bit Window systems are backward-compliant, 32-bit software will work on both 64-bit and 32-bit Windows.

Most applications will instantly determine the correct version for your machine or will run in 32-bit mode if that is the only choice available. If you've got a contemporary computer, it is almost certainly 64-bit, thus this isn't an issue. However, if you are unsure, check to see if you've got 64-bit Windows.

Once you've figured out the edition of Windows that you've got, keep a keen eye for software download links and ensure you're getting the right version for your machine. The terms x64 and x86 refer to 64-bit and 32-bit processors, respectively. It's not a good idea to install 64-bit applications on 32-bit machines since they won't work.

Run the Troubleshooters for Programs

Windows 10 comes with a number of in-built troubleshooting solutions that attempt to identify and resolve common issues. They do not often function, but they are worth a go if Windows won't let you install an application.

Go to Settings > Update & Security > Troubleshoot and select Additional troubleshooters to check out the troubleshooter for program installations. Execute your machine's Program Compatibility Troubleshooter program from this location to see if it resolves any issues.

If you're experiencing difficulties deploying a Store application, you may use the Windows Store Applications utility.

Again, if this fails to work, you may want to attempt the Uninstall Troubleshooter and Microsoft Program Install, which you can download individually.

Remove Any Earlier Editions of the Software

Running an application update (even if it is a significant new edition) usually goes without a hitch. However, having an older edition of the application installed might cause problems when trying to run the most recent edition.

If you're still having trouble installing applications on Windows, follow the route: Settings > Apps > Apps & Features and delete the latest edition. Although this should not wipe out any data you've stored in the application, it is advisable that you back up just about settings or other sensitive information beforehand, to keep it safe.

To completely delete an application, you may have to remove other elements. For example, Apple's guidelines for entirely uninstalling iTunes from Windows include instructions for uninstalling Bonjour and other applications.

Before reinstalling an app, it is a great idea to restart after removing and double-check that the program in question is indeed gone.

Examine Your Antivirus Preferences

Anti-malware or antivirus programs can oftentimes block applications from being installed on Windows. Based on the circumstances, this might be beneficial or inconvenient.

In some cases, you might well be attempting to install malicious software. When the antivirus software on your system identifies this, it should prevent you from running the program. However, if you have your antivirus alerts turned off, you may not notice this alert. To know if that's the situation, launch the Windows security suite and look for the latest warnings.

If you believe an application you intend to install includes malware, run it via a virus detector on the internet. Of course, don't install something that's contaminated. If you used to believe a software, it's conceivable that it has been hacked or that you obtained a faulty version from a dodgy source.

Nevertheless, the antivirus software might become too protective. When valid apps try installing, it may prohibit them from accessing crucial directories. If that's the matter, you'll have to turn off your antivirus for a while to allow the installation process to finish.

If you're using Microsoft Defender, check how you can turn it off if you're using the in-built solution. Most feature a setting that allows you to momentarily disable safeguards for some minutes to enable you to install what you need. Before attempting to do anything, be certain you can rely on the software!

Double-Check That the Software Is Compliant with the Windows Edition You're Using

Some apps are just incompatible with the recent Windows edition. For instance, applications built for Windows 7 that Microsoft discontinued years ago are unlikely to have been upgraded to function on Windows 11. If that's the case, Windows provides several compliance tools that can assist you in getting such programs to launch, but they may still not function correctly thereafter.

First, visit the application provider's official website to determine if the product is compatible with your Windows edition. The majority of the time, these details can be found on the support or download pages. Even if it isn't interoperable, you may still download the app installer file and try installing it, but knowing which systems are fully supported is helpful.

If the software installs successfully, run the executable and follow the instructions below. This may be done by finding the software in the Start menu bar, right-clicking it, and selecting Open file location to view it in File Explorer. If the app installer still didn't run, repeat the process using the executable.

Choose Properties from the context menu when you right-click on the file. Navigate to where the Compatibility tab is located in the resultant window. You can select an older copy of Windows to execute this software in compatibility mode. If you confirm that the program worked successfully on a previous edition, it's worth a go.

Other than that, there are additional selections under Settings, most of which are related to the presentation. In most circumstances, they aren't essential, but then, you can give them a trial to see whether they help.

If it doesn't work, you'll have to look into alternative options, such as running the earlier edition of Windows in a virtual environment.

If Windows Software is not Installing on Your System, What Should You Do?

When you are finding it hard to install programs on Windows, maybe one of the above-mentioned troubleshooting techniques will assist. This is usually due to Windows interoperability issues or the activity of security tools messing around with the installation process.

While we have concentrated on standard desktop applications, applications from Microsoft Store may also fail to install sometimes.

system. Sadly, Microsoft determined that all Windows 11 users must have the Xbox app open automatically.

Go ahead and right-click the Xbox app. To do this, locate the app in the taskbar area and click Settings from the menu to halt the operation of the app. Deselect necessary boxes in the General tab area to prevent this application from launching while you are logging in.

Remove Any Application Stubs That aren't Needed

Microsoft signed many arrangements with third-party suppliers, according to reports, to feature app stubs on the redesigned, updated Start Menu in Windows 11. Applications such as Adobe Lightroom, WhatsApp Line, and Picsart Pro to mention a few, have icons. By selecting any of these app icons, the program will be downloaded and installed.

Several Windows 11 fans might want to check out any of these programs, but mostly, these app icons will only clog up the Start Menu. You may get rid of them by clicking Uninstall from the menu when having the desired app icon right-clicked.

Do these Ten Things Right Now if You're Using Windows 11

People who fulfill the conditions may now download Windows 11 as a patch. You ought to have an action plan prepared to go in order to make the most of this upcoming transformation.

If your PC software and hardware satisfy certain requirements, Microsoft will shortly upgrade Windows 10 customers to Windows 11. Although you can prevent the transition, this upgrade is essentially not elective—it'll occur as an aspect of a routine, planned update.

Because the upgrade to Windows 11 is virtually unavoidable, it is critical to be prepared for the change when it comes. While the majority of the Windows 11 upgrade will focus on safety, there are a minimum of eleven user interface, settings, and app changes that'll require rapid user response and life quality adjustments.

Make the Xbox App Not Launch When You Log In

When Windows 11 first loaded up, the very first thing you'll see is a giant advertising page encouraging you to register for a Game Pass with the Xbox app. Although this is not always the case. For some users, the Xbox app is something that they'll not always want to run on their

Remove Any Programs That Clog Up Your Taskbar, Such as Widgets

Also, you need to apply some cutbacks to the taskbar to complement the removal of superfluous programs and application stubs from your Start Menu.

It's not necessary to attach all of those app icons to the taskbar. Widgets, for instance, is a taskbar program that is completely optional. You might say the same thing about Messenger, based on the way you utilize your computer. Have a free portion of the taskbar right-clicked, choose settings, then slide the corresponding icons to the Off state to eliminate those two programs.

Look Out for App Updates

When you get a significant Microsoft update, you should go above and beyond to look for any further updates. It's often possible that the corporation has released a follow-up to the follow-up. All you have to do is to carry out a fast inspection of the Update & Security settings page.

Include Useful Applications that are Missing

Microsoft opted to eliminate a major program from Windows Start Menu that average Windows operators would notice straight away after they install Windows 11 on their PC—PowerShell. The ability to quickly switch from the conventional Windows Terminal to PowerShell from the Start Menu checklist appears to have been removed as well.

To install PowerShell programs to your Start Menu of your Windows 11PC, type the app's name into the search box and then have it attached to the taskbar or menu. The program icons will be added to the Start Menu's end, where you may relocate them towards a more obvious location if desired.

Verify your Privacy Configurations

Although the privacy configurations that you made in Windows 10 should've been moved to Windows 11, it's a good idea to double-check them to ensure they still represent your desires. Those setup options may be found in the Windows Settings menu.

Many Windows customers are fine with exchanging their search histories and activity metrics with Microsoft and anyone who could have access to the details, while others aren't.

Verify the state of activation

Another parameter that really should have escaped the upgrade to Windows 11 from Windows 10 was the operating system's activation status. Nevertheless, it's a good idea to double-check this on the

Windows 11 System Settings Screen, which can be found in the Activation section.

Make the UI Unique to You

Several Windows 11's revamped user interface conventions might not attract all of us, but that is a question of personal choice. There are simply too many customization options in Windows 11 to enumerate here.

Customization also encompasses backdrop pictures, font, themes, and colors, as well as personal preferences. Maybe it is time to modify the general design of your UI to coincide with the upgrade to Windows 11?

Verify That All Peripherals Are in Good Working Order

It's likely that accessibility to a few of your endpoints didn't escape the changeover, as it does with every Windows OS upgrade. you verify if there is a requirement for fresh drivers or if you only have to reconnect your wireless connectivity.

You can monitor the availability of your peripherals by traversing to the Devices and Bluetooth section of your Windows 11 Settings application.

Check for App Compliance

You might be restricted access to some of your peripheral devices as well as interoperability with critical apps while upgrading to Windows 11 from Windows 10. To verify that all key programs are operating correctly following the upgrade, they should be tested.

Not Everyone Has Access to Windows 11

As previously stated, the prerequisites for updating to Windows 11 from Windows 10 are extensive and carefully implemented. It's likely that your reasonably nice Windows 10 computer, even if it's just a couple of years, will fall short of the requirements. You want to take one careful look at the Windows Update page in the System Settings area to be pretty sure.

If your computer doesn't meet the minimum specifications, the tech giant will make the reason clear to you and, if feasible, offer advice on how to meet it. Sadly, a large chunk of Windows users will discover that their machines cannot and do not fulfill the minimum requirements for their Windows 11 computer.

Three Ways of Installing Windows 11 on Computers That Are Not Supported

Updating your computer to the most recent edition of Windows is a good idea if you want to stay updated with the current developments, however, unlike the earlier edition of Windows, this upgrade is somewhat pompous.

Installing Windows 11 on older computers, such as a 2nd Generation computer featuring legacy BIOS can be a hell of a challenge.

In this section of this eBook, we'll show you how you can install Windows 11 on your computers, even if they are not supported. Hence, if you've got a fairly old computer that Windows 11 installation didn't pull through, or if you'd like to impose the installation of Windows 11 on your old computer to enable you to try out all those mouth-watering features you've read about the new operating system, then you want to employ the methods below. And rest assured that we've only chosen techniques that won't hurt your computer or cause data loss.

Recognize Computer Limitations that aren't Supported

Although Windows 11 could indeed run on the majority of unsupported PCs, it does not guarantee that it will run flawlessly. Some capabilities may find it hard functioning properly, or Windows might become corrupted or misfire, depending on which system type you are operating. Microsoft advises against installing this new operating system on unsupported gadgets since such gadgets cannot be guaranteed to get all future upgrades.

So, keep these considerations in mind when installing the new operating system on your unsupported computer, since no single person will be liable for any device or data loss.

Enable Secure Boot and TPM 2.0

Before we teach you how to install this new operating system on your unsupported endpoint, you want to ensure that your computer is unsupported. The absence of Secure Boot and TPM 2.0 support is the most common cause of unsupported errors on the latest computers.

These two systems are typically available on PCs, but they are turned off by default. All you have to do now is activate them before attempting to install the new operating system.

Sadly, we won't offer specific instructions for enabling both of these choices because they're activated in your device's BIOS, and this varies by manufacturer. However, we will present steps that ought to work for the majority of computers.

To go into the BIOS, hit the DEL, F1, F12, F2, or F10 key continuously while the computer is booting up. Depending on your computer maker, you'll have to hit a different key. The F12 button is used, for instance, in HP computers.

Secure Boot and TPM 2.0 may be found on the Security page as soon as you're there. Secure Boot may be found in the Boot options menu on some computers. To implement the modifications, be sure to close the BIOS with the "Save changes and exit" selected.

Download the ISO file for Windows 11

To use the following procedures, you'll need to have an ISO file for Windows 11. If you're yet to try out Windows 11 installation on your PC, or if you've used the media creation of the operating system rather than the ISO to make a bootable device, then there's a need to have the ISO file of Windows 11 downloaded to use the techniques discussed below.

The ISO file for Windows 11 may be simply downloaded from Microsoft's official website. Simply scroll down to the Windows 11 Disk Image Download part and hit the Download option. After you are done with that, you'll have to choose which Windows language you want to use to acquire the download URL.

Method 1: Bypass the required check by editing the registry

If you wouldn't bother fiddling with the Windows Registry, then this is the simplest approach that doesn't need the use of third-party products. By adding an item in the Registry, you may prohibit Windows 11 from verifying various requirements, contingent on your device.

Based on what characteristics your computer already has, you'll need to create various entries. We'll discuss them in more detail in the following sections:

> **Caution:** Making a mistake in the Registry might cause problems for your computers, such as data loss or Windows corruption. Hence, you can either back up the Registry manually or utilize a registry housekeeper to restore and back it up automatically before effecting the modifications discussed below.

Circumvent CPU and TPM 2.0 Requirement Assessment

If your computer comes with TPM 1.2 enabled but no TPM 2.0 enabled or CPU requirement assessment, you'll have to perform the following registry change:

Utilizing the search field on Windows or running commands by holding down the Windows + R buttons and inputting the term "Regedit" in the Run dialog, you can easily access the Registry.

Please go to this area. HKEY_LOCAL_MACHINE > SYSTEM > Setup > MoSetup. Also, you can directly navigate to this place by copying and pasting the address below into the provided search box atop the Windows Registry window.

\HKEY_LOCAL_MACHINE\SYSTEM\Setup\MoSetup

Right-click, using your mouse, on any empty white area in the right pane while you get busy selecting the MoSetup folder, and choose DWORD Value.

There will be a new entry generated.

AllowUpgradesWithUnsupportedTPMOrCPU, for example, should be named AllowUpgradesWithUnsupportedTPMOrCPU, and it should be set to 1.

Now you can have Windows 11 installed with the aid of bootable USB drives or a loaded ISO file. The CPU and TPM 2.0 limitations will not be an issue.

Circumvent Secure Boot or TPM Check

You'll have to make two registry changes if your computer doesn't support Secure Boot and TPM. Let's take a look at how you can achieve this:

Navigate to HKEY_LOCAL_MACHINE > SYSTEM > Setup in system Registry. You may also paste/copy the path below into the search field of the Registry:

\HKEY_LOCAL_MACHINE\SYSTEM\Setup

Start a fresh entry in the Setup area by right-clicking it and selecting New > Key. Title the new item LabConfig. Right-click on a free area in the right-hand panel when LabConfig is chosen and choose DWORD Value.

Rename the value to 00000001 by retitling it BypassTPMCheck and double-clicking it. The TPM inspection will be disabled as a result of this, but the Secure Boot inspection will require a separate entry.

Choose DWORD Value when right-clicking in the free white area in LabConfig. Double-click BypassSecureBootCheck, give it a designation, and have its value set to 00000001.

Secure Boot and TPM 2.0 won't be checked while Windows 11 is installed on your device.

Method 2: Prepare a bootable USB Drive with no Prerequisites

You may also generate a bootable DVD or USB drive for Windows 11 that will not verify Secure Boot or TPM 2.0 support if you wouldn't like to or can't change the Registry. This technique is also preferable if you'd like to run Windows 11 on a number of unsupported computers because you will not have to change each one to render it Windows 11-compliant.

Rufus, a renowned bootable USB drive program, will be required for this. Rufus' creators have released a great method for producing Windows 11 bootable USBs that disables the functionality that scans for Secure Boot and TPM capability. Below is how you can put it to use:

- Ensure you've got the ISO file for Windows 11 before downloading Rufus.
- Run the Rufus program after plugging in a USB disk with a minimum of eight gigabytes of empty space. The associated USB disk will be picked.
- Choose Select in the Boot options section, then locate and run the ISO file of Windows 11 that you just downloaded.

- There will be a fresh Image options area. Click Extended Windows 11 Installation from the drop-down menu.
- After that, contingent on your computer's drive partition structure, choose GPT or MBR.
- The remnant of the parameters is optional to render this functional, but if have the tiniest idea of what you're doing, you can modify them.
- The program will now build a bootable USB disk without checking for Secure Boot or TPM compatibility if you press the START option. You can use it to improve your existing system or a different PC.

Method 3: Edit a Bootable USB Stick for Windows 10

This procedure is tough and error-prone, but it is just about the only way to get Windows 11 installed on old machines featuring legacy BIOS. We'll alter a bootable USB drive of Windows 10 to have Windows 11 installed rather than Windows 10. The installer program will believe it is trying to install Windows 10 and will look for the same prerequisites, but it'll actually be installing Windows 11.

Before we explain the procedure, you must be aware that you can only use it to update your present Windows edition. It is not feasible for installing Windows 11 in dual-boot arrangements or for booting computers from a USB drive.

Using this method, you'll be able to update to both Windows 7 and Windows 10 effectively. If you're using a dual-boot system, ensure that you do it in the Windows edition you'll like to upgrade. We're guessing that you've got the ISO file of Windows 11 ready, so all you have now is a bootable USB device for Windows 10.

Attach an eight-gigabyte or larger USB disk to your computer and download the media creation application for Windows 10 to create a bootable Windows 10 disk. This program will go ahead and download Windows 10 into your device and generate a bootable disk for you instantly.

As soon as you've created a bootable USB, you want to follow the instructions below precisely as we suggest.

- **Step 1**: First, you must mount the Windows 11 ISO image. Right-click the ISO file and choose Mount on Windows 8, 8.1, or 10. You'll have to utilize third-party installation programs such as WinCDEmu on previous editions.

- **Step 2**: As soon as Windows 11 is mounted, navigate to the sources folder and copy the file titled install.wim.
- **Step 3**: In your File Explorer, launch the Windows 10 bootable USB disk and navigate to the same folder.
- **Step 4**: Delete the install.esd file and replace it with the file you named install.wim earlier which you also copied. If Windows complains that this file is enormously too large to transfer, you have to convert the USB drive to the NTFS storage system.
- **Step 5**: From the USB device, launch the setup file of Windows 10.
- **Step 6**: Choose Not right now from the download updates selection of Change how Windows Setup.
- **Step 7**: Select Next, and you'll be prompted by Windows to agree to some conditions before informing you of what edition of Windows 11 will be installed on your device and the data that you want to preserve.
- **Step 8**: Once you've made your choice, Windows will begin the process of installation then reboot your computer after it is done with it. When it reboots, you'll be given the option of upgrading your present Windows or installing it on a fresh disk. Ensure you choose to update to the most recent version of Windows.

That is all there is to it. The installation of Windows will begin. Furthermore, despite the fact that the procedure says "install Windows 10," what you'll actually get o your system at the end of the day is Windows 11.

Note that because this is an unapproved hack, you can't have Windows 11 installed by booting your computer with the USB. It is for this reason that, when prompted after the reboot, we advise that you choose to update your current Windows rather than install it on a new disk. Else, it'll spit out a disk error message, requiring you to repeat the procedure from within Windows.

The second technique is ideal because it can perform all the complicated work effortlessly and will not make any modifications to your computer. If nothing else works, the third option should be if your computer is capable of installing and deploying Windows 10.

Windows 11 System Requirements

These are the minimum system requirements for Windows 11 installation on computers. If your machine does not match these criteria, you will be unable to run Windows 11 and should consider acquiring a new computer.

To upgrade, your computer must have Windows 10, the 2004 edition, or later versions. Windows Update, found under Settings>Update and Security, provides your system with free software updates.

- **Processor**: 1 gigahertz (GHz) or higher on a suitable 64-bit CPU or SoC (System on a Chip) with dual or additional cores.
- **RAM**: 4GB
- **Storage:** Storage device with a capacity of 64 GB or more.
- **System Firmware**: An UEFI-compliant Secure Boot.
- **TPM:** Comes with TPM (Trusted Platform Module) version 2.0.
- **Graphics Card**
- With the WDDM 2.0 driver function, it's compliant with DirectX 12 or newer editions.
- **Display**
- HD display that is higher than nine inches diagonally, eight bits for each color channel.

Transition to Windows is Totally Free!

One of the recurring questions that intending Windows 11 users ask is whether they have to pay anything to use it.

Windows 11 is surprisingly a no-charge upgrade for anyone who has already installed Windows 10. So, irrespective of if your computer is technically enabled or not, if you are using Windows 10 Pro or Home on it, you can install and enable the corresponding version of Windows 11.

Chapter 2: What is Interface?

An interface is an application, webpage, or device that facilitates computer-human interactions. Screen displays, a mouse, a keyboard, and the look of your PC's desktop are all examples of this. Users can successfully operate their PC or gadget they're working with thanks to user interfaces. A great interface should be simple, quick, and easy to use. This brings us to the following section.

What are the Most Crucial Components of a UI?

The bits we employ to develop responsive applications and websites are known as UI elements. They give the user contact points like checkboxes, menu items, scrollbars, and buttons as they find their path around. Typically, user interface components come in our classes:

- *Input Controls*

Users can enter data into their PC via input controls. If system operators want to inform their acquaintance about the region that they're in, for instance, they'll require the services of input controls.

- *Navigation Elements*

Users can travel across a website or product with the use of navigational elements. Tab panels on iOS smartphones and a hamburger panel on Android gadgets are popular navigational elements.

- *Informational Elements*

Users can access information from informational elements. Pop-up windows, message boxes, progress bars, and notifications are all examples of this.

- *Containers*

Containers, like accordions, keep related material grouped. A vertically grouped items list with hiding/show capabilities is known as an accordion.

User Interfaces Types

As implied earlier, the user interface is an area where computers and people communicate; it comprises information produced from the device and a collection of control systems that allow the operator to conduct specific tasks. These exchanges result in a seamless system in which computers assist the operator in making decisions and the operator, in return, can efficiently run it. The objective while creating the user interface is to design it in a user-friendly and self-explanatory manner so that operators can get the outcomes they want fast.

Because many organizations are becoming increasingly reliant on online and mobile apps, proper user interface design is becoming increasingly important. In this section, we'll be looking at the many types of UIs and their benefits and drawbacks. Also, we'll look at the interaction between operators and various types of UIs to assist you to grasp when to utilize which one.

Graphical UI

The Benefits of Using a Graphical UI

- Non-technical operators will find it useful.
- Operators are unaware of the intricacy of activities.
- Appealing images augment the look.
- Instantaneous visual response

- Makes use of actual-world models and images
- Allows for the use of numerous input devices

Using a Graphical UI Has Its Drawbacks

- Needs a lot of memory and power
- There's a chance it'll be hard to find.
- The increasing number of control components may overwhelm users.
- It is necessary to seek hidden directives on purpose.

Helpful Hints

It's complicated to handle graphical UIs. Numerous panels and other GUI-specific aspects, like mouse and keyboard interactions, are common in this style of the user interface.

It should operate swiftly and reliably, consume a reasonable number of processors, contain primarily intelligible parts for novice operators, and fulfill a variety of other criteria. It should contain a comprehensive handbook devoted to the system's operations, including which item on the menu links to which location.

The following are some of the qualities that'll be beneficial to you:

- A universal search for settings and functions
- Tooltips for button icons and menu items
- Different sorts of menus are used to separate software functions (drop-down menu, quick-access buttons, pop-up menu).

You don't need to invent anything from the beginning because there are lots of publications on the subject that describe tried and proven procedures.

Touchscreen Graphical UI

Operators communicate with their gadgets using their fingertips when using gadgets using Touchscreen Graphical UI. Because of the prominence of smartphones and tablets, this has become a popular pick. When you glance at practically any content on your tablet or smartphone, you'll encounter a touchscreen graphical user interface.

Click, swiping (typically analogous to right-clicking the mouse), and certain additional functionalities, such as a two-finger-touch motion to rotate/zoom an item, are the key variations from regular GUI.

Overall, operators may choose from a variety of pointing movements, including duration of motion, velocity change, direction change, absence of movement, endpoints and path start, tapping, pointing, time-based movements, and looping.

The Benefits of a Graphical UI on a Touchscreen

- It's faster and easier than typing or using a mouse.
- Doesn't utilize peripherals like a mouse or keyboard.
- The addition of numerous movement actions is possible.
- Suitable for both youngsters and the elderly
- Zoom-in movements make it easier for visually challenged people to use the computer.
- Compatibility with a variety of gadgets

Using a Touchscreen Graphical UI Has Its Drawbacks

The amount of control components is restricted by the size of the mobile display.

- Additional movements may be difficult to locate.
- Can be initiated unintentionally by accidental touches

> **Helpful Hints**
>
> With the exception of forms that need typing numerous texts, which is unpleasant for operators, touchscreen Graphical UI may be utilized in a number of ways. Use user interface components that operate as buttons, such as bullet-select and drop-down select, switch, and lots more.
>
> It's also crucial to scale correctly. On larger screens, user interface components shouldn't appear bloated; but, on tinier gadgets, operators should have the capacity to easily touch the keys. To avoid inadvertent clicks, ensure the buttons are spaced away. Finally, apply touch-centered design principles like swipe-to-delete or left-swiping to access the menu.

Menu-Driven User Interface

A sequence of panels, or "menus," is used in menu-driven user interfaces. When an operator taps or clicks on a list format or graphic, it advances to the following menu display until the intended result is achieved.

The menu preferences on your smartphone are an instance. You can only browse through the preferences and touch things; there's no other way to engage. As a result, it's employed in apps that have a simple, limited, and consistent set of functionalities. You may group them together under names such as "Display Settings," "Camera Settings" and so on.

Benefits of a Menu-Driven User Interface

- Ideal for novices and inexperienced computer operators.
- Operators have a low mental burden.
- Consistent user interface across systems
- You're in control of establishing a structure and sequence for user paths.
- You have more flexibility over how users connect with you.
- Easy to integrate with a variety of gadgets

The Drawbacks of a Menu-Driven User Interface

- Menu selections are minimal.
- Submenus may be hard to locate.
- The dangers of picking up too much display space or being too little
- Needs additional steps for a basic activity.

> **Helpful Hints**
>
> Due to its restrictions, menus are a relatively intuitive interface. You may scroll all the way to the top to obtain a general concept of what is attainable. This is, however, what you may hypothetically develop. In reality, it is possible to make a mistake. You might establish a menu with headers such as Customization, Tools, Parameters, and Settings, but it will be useless to you. There's no explanation for what headings accomplish or why there are four of them for what appears to be the same activity. The menu layout should be well-designed to enable you easily figure out where they'll take you. Or else, the user experience will worsen, and you'll be forced to browse all the items on the menu in order to locate the correct one.

The CLI (Command Line Interface)

A CLI is a low-level text-centered UI for dealing with a computer. This style of menu is often not meant for the ordinary user. It's most commonly utilized while interacting with cloud-based computer systems or executing administrator duties.

Numerous services and programs have a command-line interface aside from a graphical user interface to help automate chores. It may be difficult to push buttons in the GUI while utilizing bots or interacting between apps. It's a lot simpler to tell your PC to execute a certain console command.

A terminal on any OS is an illustration of a command-line interface that most users are acquainted with (Linux, macOS, and Windows).

The Benefits of Using a CLI

- More responsive than other forms of user interfaces
- Processing needs on the CPU are reduced.
- Can be used with a display with a lower resolution.
- It may easily be scaled up or down in size.
- Ability to combine many operations into a single command
- The ability to accomplish complex tasks by triggering cross-app connections

Cons of Using a CLI

- Experience or/and coding abilities are required.
- Errors are caused by mistakes in command syntax.

- Typically takes input from the keyboard.
- It's not intuitive — you'll need to study the handbook before you can use it.

Helpful Hints

Take into account your intended audience while creating a CLI - individuals who've got some expertise using consoles. System admins, programmers, and frequent operators of Unix-centered systems are among the intended audience.

Even advanced operators, however, will want some assistance to find out how to utilize the application. Because CLI is not the least appealing sort of user interface, ensure that your terminal commands have tutorials and manuals.

Also, it is critical to provide proper error handling. It should send an error report if you provide inadequate inputs to the command or commit syntax errors. The alert should include enough details to pinpoint the exact location of the issue as well as a manual guide with a demonstration of how to utilize it.

Conversational User Interface

Contemporary technology is majorly graphic, but the conversational user interface makes use of language and words-based interaction, which is just as important, if not even more than visual interaction. Operators may engage with devices just by instructing them on what they should do using conversational user interfaces. It can be spoken, voice-activated, or typed. To use the first kind, the program must be able to recognize voices.

Contingent on the device's sophistication, it may accept more formal input like "notify me tomorrow" or more informal questions.

The introduction of this tech meant that operators could converse with their devices in a sentient manner rather than utilizing system-specific terminology. This interface is equipped with learning and self-teaching capabilities, making it more helpful the more you are using it.

Benefits of a Conversational User Interface

- There isn't a need to acquire new capabilities.
- The voice adds to the realism.
- Makes a personal connection with operators
- Responds to circumstances in order to create a connection.
- Recognizes speech rate, accent, tone, and gender.
- It's possible to include it in current apps.

- The Drawbacks of Conversational User Interfaces

- Textual and visual clues are few.

- It's possible that expressing orders will be difficult.

Helpful Hints

You don't want to become stuck in a verbal rut. Else, you'll be disappointed by their incapacity to utilize the program, or angry that the creators failed to account for all possible dialogue results. They're less probable to utilize the service once more in either circumstance.

Make your messages as brief as possible. Even when you feel compelled to respond with a lot of details, you risk overloading your operators. The discourse should be based on a turn-taking system that'll allow them to talk seamlessly.

Make use of the user interface's personality traits and tone in its actions and words. Operators will find the UI more appealing with indirect characterization. Since humans are pre-programmed to allocate personas.

A great UI should be simple to utilize, have easy-to-understand user paths, let operators experiment with different choices, be attractive to the eye, utilize appropriate colors for critical places, and assist with the documentation.

Assess what your operators require and what will streamline your app's procedures to decide what's best. For some, syntax-specific instructions or touching buttons will suffice, while others will feel that communicating to a PC is the most comfortable method of engagement.

Many programmers fall into a trap of creating technology applications without considering the social aspects of engagement. A conversational user interface, on the flip side, allows you to engage with the machine on human understanding and language.

New UI and Design

The new interface design is the very first feature you'll discover when you install Windows 11. Every user interface component and the window now have curved edges, thanks to a redesign by Microsoft.

This holds for both the context menu and the File Explorer. Some people aren't delighted with this new context menu feature in Windows 11, but then you can turn it off if you wish.

File Explorer has undergone significant improvements, and it now appears to be a lot smoother than it was previously. The Ribbons have been replaced with a modern and streamlined toolbar that contains the most often used commands.

This is a significant improvement over the File Explorer feature in Windows 10, and the redesigned UI is less crowded while still giving you the most important selections. To top things off, there is a new icons collection to choose from. These are not the sole improvements; the Taskbar and Start Menu have been completely redesigned, and they now have a cleaner, more simplified appearance.

The Taskbar has been centralized, and it resembles that of Chrome OS or macOS. If you don't like the new Start Menu, you could always relocate it to the left-hand side in the Settings application. Sadly, unlike past editions, the Taskbar is now fixed at the base and cannot be moved to the side or top.

The Start Menu has also been updated, and it now has curved sides like the rest of the windows. Also, you will observe that the Start Menu has been simplified and has lesser apps.

There is now a dedicated applications area that allows users access to their favorite applications swiftly and conveniently. A suggested section appears underneath it, which you may utilize to browse recently accessed files or newly installed programs.

All of your applications are still visible, but they're now buried at the back of the All Apps icon. In comparison to the Windows 10 equivalent, the redesigned Start Menu appears to be much more ordered and basic. The Notification Center has also been completely redesigned, with a Notifications bar and Quick Settings option replacing the Action Center.

This implies that fast settings are no longer bundled with notifications and may be seen alone. The two fresh panels have curved edges to fit the new Windows 11 style.

Just as importantly, with Windows 11, Microsoft Edge received a redesign that has minimalistic and a basic UI. We prefer the new Windows 11 appearance, but if you don't like it, you can easily change it to be seen as the Windows 10 interface.

Widgets

Live Tiles have been deprecated in Windows 11 in favor of widgets that provide the same function. Despite their similarities, they do not live on the Start Menu and rather feature their panel. This appears to be a fantastic addition, and because widgets have got their specific panel, they will not consume as much area as Live Tiles previously did.

User Interface

Shadows, translucency, a redesigned color palette, and curved geometry are all featured all through the OS, which is based on the Fluent Design System. The look dubbed as "Mica," is defined as a "dynamic, opaque, material that integrates desktop wallpaper and theme to color the backdrop of long-lived panels including such settings and applications," is a prominent feature of the layout. The start menu and much of the UI are heavily influenced by the now-defunct Windows 10X.

The buttons of the taskbar are centrally positioned by design, and it is irrevocably fixed to the screen's bottom edge; unlike earlier editions of Windows, you cannot move it to the right, left, or upper sides of the display. Quick Actions toggles, media playback controls, brightness, and volume, have been relocated to a different configuration pop-up revealed by hitting the system tray.

Task View, new functionality in Windows 10, has a new look and allows you to assign different backgrounds for every virtual desktop. Two new capabilities have been added to the window snapping features: "snap layouts" lets the operator choose a predetermined arrangement for tiling several windows on a screen. As just a "snap group," the patterned layout of windows may be shrunk and recovered from the taskbar.

The Segoe user interface font has been changed to a dynamic version, allowing it to adapt better across different screen resolutions. New system symbols, anime, audio, and widgets are among the other improvements.

Start Menu

This new Start menu is a simpler edition of the one seen in Windows 10, but it does not have Live Tiles. Pinnable applications recently used files, and the option to swiftly restart or shut down 11 computers are all included. It's much more straightforward than what's available in Windows 10 right now.

If you wouldn't like the Start menu and program icons to be centralized, you can drag them all back to the left. When combined with the dark mode, Windows 11 begins to resemble a more polished edition of Windows 10 rather than anything entirely new. The Start menu in Windows 11 can be moved to the left-hand side.

Microsoft has used curved edges in Windows 11 as well. These may be found in context menus, applications, and the File Explorer. Rounded edges can also be found on the Start menu.

More modifications to the in-built programs are expected in Windows 11, although most of them don't seem to be available yet.

The Windows 11 File Explorer

The Windows 11 File Explorer is nearly identical to File Explorer in Windows 10 in terms of functionality: It's a paneled display that allows you to work with some of your PC's files. However, there have been some changes to how you do that task.

Close buttons, maximize, and minimize, navigation buttons, a toolbar, a sidebar, a search bar, and a path bar, and the main section from where you can modify how the files are listed out are all there.

All File Explorer windows in Windows 11 have curved sides, a redesigned toolbar, and lots of files and programs have new symbols. You'll also notice that the right-click menu bar is modified.

A Brand-New Toolbar

When contrasted with Windows 10, the File Explorer in Windows 11 has a significantly reduced toolbar. The tabbed "View," "Edit," and "File" choices are no longer available in the sophisticated, segmented ribbon display. In its stead are a set of simple icons that allow you to do basic operations (including creating new folders, copying, pasting, renaming, and deleting), sort icons, and alter the display in the window.

For overflowing elements like charting a network drive, choosing all objects in the display, and accessing options, there also are ellipses (three-dotted) panels.

Although concealing options may oftentimes make a display more difficult to utilize, Microsoft appears to have achieved the correct balance in this situation.

A Similar Sidebar

Each File Explorer panel in Windows 11 has a sidebar that works almost similar to the 10's sidebar. It allows you to pin objects, move them about with your mouse, and get swift access to specific folders, disks, and network shares.

Streamlined Right-Click Menu

The fresh right-click menu in the File Explorer Windows 11 is one of the most notable departures from convention. When you right-click icons, you can see a variety of icons that depict basic actions like paste, copy, cut, delete, and rename. These icons have been laid down in a sequence from Windows 95 to Windows 10.

New Icons

Nearly every single major Windows edition has been accompanied by a new collection of icons. Windows 11 is not different, as it comes with a new set of bright icons with a shaded, flat style for its in-built programs. Updated File Explorer icons indicate general documents, folders, and specific folders such as "Downloads" and "Picture," among other things.

The Desktop

The Windows 11 desktop is almost identical to the Windows 10 desktop. It's a specific directory that may store files, directories, and shortcuts, exactly like every other Windows version since Windows 95. All icons are visible in different sizes, much as in Windows 10, by using the right-click option or dragging your mouse scroll wheel while pressing Ctrl.

Dark Mode

Windows 11 provides the freedom to pick a darkish desktop theme, which is visually pleasing in dark situations, similar to Windows 10. You'll get a beautiful viewing experience when you mix it with a dark edition of the desktop background of Windows 11 (thanks to the

Windows 11 dark mode under the Settings > Personalization > Themes route).

Folder Options

There're lots of historical dialogs hiding behind the curtains in the Windows 11 Insider Preview, so don't expect everything to be brand new. An outstanding demonstration is the Options menu. If you choose "Options" from the toolbar's ellipses icon (triple points), you'll get a "Folder Options" box that appears remarkably comparable to what is obtainable in Windows 10, although with some new icons supplanting previous ones. (Also, the Folder Options box is not compliant with the Dark Mode in the original version.)

Windows Widget

Widgets are a collection of tiny visual programs that you can access straight from the taskbar of Windows 11 and are intended to give immediate details about stocks, sports results, weather, news, etc. You can modify the widget menu to display just the widgets you like, and it also contains a Bing search functionality that opens results in a separate browser tab.

Anyone who has made use of the Live Tiles features in Windows 10, or more lately, the News and Interests panel, will recognize the appearance and basic information delivery method of the widgets in Windows 11.

However, widgets seem to have some parallels to the "gadgets" function in Windows 7 and Vista, which allowed users to include tiny icons that displayed information such as weather and news headlines before Microsoft removed it due to safety concerns over third-party devices.

Widgets, on the other hand, is driven entirely by Microsoft services like the Edge browser and MSN, safe for the time being.

How to Create Folders And Documents?

There's a fresh right-click option for File Explorer and the desktop in Windows 11. The desktop's right-click menu is located somewhere on the left-hand side. The right-click button in File Explorer is what you should use.

Sure, you may create a fresh folder or file in Windows 11 by right-clicking the File Explorer or the desktop and selecting New. However, with the File Explorer option, you may utilize a new approach to do this task. Below are two ways of creating folders and files on your Windows 11 PC.

Using the File Explorer

We're going to create a fresh Word document.

- Utilize the New Button that is located somewhere in the Ribbon Menu
- Go to the folder where you want to make a file and open it.
- Inside this new folder, choose the arrow down button.
- Select **New > Microsoft** Word from the drop-down menu.
- Finish the file creation process by giving the file a name and clicking another space.

Making Use of the Universal Approach

- Go to the folder where you'd like to make a fresh folder and open it.
- Select **New > Folder** from the context menu of the empty area by right-clicking it.
- In your Windows 11 PC's File Explorer, type a word for the folder and then click a free space to create it.
- In Windows 11 PC's File Explorer, utilize the universal approach to make a fresh folder.

How to Recover Lost and Deleted /Folder/Files in Your Windows 11 PC

If you accidentally erase essential folders or files and want to recover them, the internet is filled with recovery tools that can be of assistance. You want to hop on your browser and carry out a quick research on these tools and keep them handy in the event that you mistakenly delete your file or folder. Some of these tools are completely free programs. It may be used to recover a variety of files and folders from hard disks.

You may start this program after installing it on your PC and selecting the drive from which you'd like to restore the data to scan. After you are done scanning your drive, go through the scan results for files and folders that you'd still like to use and pick them to restore back to your system. You now understand how you can use the New Folder option or the universal way in the creation of a new folder or file in your Windows 11 PC's File Explorer. You may just choose your chosen method of completing the task. Windows 11 is the latest version of the Windows OS.

How to Open Applications?

Microsoft hasn't given up on the Start Menu yet. The Windows 8's Start Menu was a complete failure, and it quickly turned out to be one of the operating system's most vehement critiques. Microsoft had to 'correct' it ultimately, but Windows 11 now includes a revamped Start Menu that differs from those in Windows 7, Windows 8, and Windows 10. There'll be a period of adjustment for operators, as well as some animosity.

Windows 11 Application List

The Windows 11 Start Menu 11 is redesigned, but it still has an Apps list, which lists all of the applications that have been installed on the machine. Operators may launch an application by clicking on it. The key is to figure out how you can find yourself in the Applications list.

Opening Applications List on Windows 11

Since the revamped Start Menu in Window 11 still displays pinned programs, the Applications list is easily accessible but just not as effortless to discover.

How to Adjust the Saturation and Contrast of Your PC's Display

- To access the Start Menu, hit the Windows or Start button situated on the taskbar.

91

- In the upper right-hand side of the display, choose All Apps.

- The Applications list will appear. Pick an application to launch by scrolling through it.

Applications List Speed Dial

As implied earlier, the Windows 11 Start Menu has been redesigned, although it retains many of the same functions as the Start Menu in Windows 10. The speed dial function has been retained. You may access the speed dial by clicking a character in the applications list, such as A. If you select a distinct character, such as if, you will be sent to a category of programs that begin with the alphabet F. It renders browsing a lot more convenient.

Getting The Start Menu of Windows 10 in Windows 11

In Windows 11, a registry workaround was capable of restoring the Start Menu in Windows. Microsoft has stopped it, despite the fact that it performed at the period. This is not surprising, and it's probable to result in a slew of additional registry-based adjustments uncovered as Windows 11 is still in development. When Windows 11 is released to the general population, it'll function significantly different than it does today in its preview version.

title

In Windows 11, the Start Menu is separated into parts, with pinned programs showing at the head of a browsable list. Because this area is browsable, anchoring an application in the Start Menu will lose part of its functionality. When you've got a lot of applications attached to your PC's Start menu, they'll display on the subsequent 'page,' requiring operators to browse to launch. Folders and application groups have also been deleted.

Chapter 3: What are Web Browsers?

The internet, which was formerly primarily utilized for education and business, is now used for every other thing from teleconferencing to shopping to surveying to gaming with your family and friends. While almost anyone can think of making use of the internet, not everyone truly understands its modus operandi. Let's take a look at one of the basic tools for navigating the world wide web: an internet browser.

An internet browser often called a browser or web browser is a piece of technology that allows users to have some access to the internet. It is a one-click portal to the totality of human thought and knowledge, allowing you to look up the solution to any query. You can explore any webpage and simply transverse to other websites using browsers, just like you can explore shops at the market and stay in those you enjoy before continuing with the other.

Examples of Web Browsers

It's just as crucial to have a phone number and home address as it is to have access to the internet. As a result, nearly every smartphone, tablet, and PC have internet access and browser.

To provide you with an understanding of the numerous types of browsers accessible, we'll look at some of the most common ones in the industry.

Google Chrome

Google Chrome remains the most used browser in the world, with a 70% market share. Chrome's success is due in part to its quick surfing speeds and simple connection with your Google profile, rendering it among the handiest browser for most users out there. Google Chrome is exceptionally easy to refashion and personalize since it has the greatest collection of addons among the major web browsers.

Safari

All Apple products, including iPhones, iPads, and Macs, use Safari as their standard internet browser. While the majority of users do not own a Mac laptop, plenty does own iPads and iPhones. In fact, in the United States, Safari remains the most widely used smartphone browser. While utilizing a PC is definitely superior to using a smartphone or tablet, Safari's appearance and experience are identical across all Apple products.

Microsoft Edge

Microsoft Edge is the company's new premier browser, substituting the outdated and old Internet Explorer. Any gadget running Microsoft's Windows OS has this internet browser by default. Microsoft Edge is based on Chromium internet technology, which also serves as the foundation for Google Chrome and a host of other browsers.

Mozilla Firefox

Firefox was formerly one of the most famous internet browser software in the United States, and it was the heir to Netscape Navigator, which was one of the first hugely available internet browsers. However, Safari and Chrome have lately gained market share. Notwithstanding its decline in popularity, Mozilla Firefox still has a small but dedicated user base and offers browser functionality comparable to its well-known rivals.

One explanation for Firefox's longevity is because it is based on an open-source framework and includes open-source tools that make it simple for programmers and other online pros to check and upgrade their sites for usability, privacy, and security upgrades.

Opera

Despite never being the most famous browser, Opera has maintained a consistent user base throughout time. This is partly due to the browser's unique capabilities, which include an ad blocker and in-built proxy.

What is the Best Way to Utilize a Browser?

For a small company owner, the Internet provides nearly endless opportunities. Getting online, whether it's for a basic informational webpage to market your business or a full-fledged eCommerce retail with shopping carts, might be the initial move in a fresh start for your company. Start by opening your laptop's web browser and reacquainting yourself with the worldwide web.

- To open the Start menu, select the Windows **"Start"** icon on the bottom left-hand side of your display.

- Select **"All Programs"** from the drop-down menu to get a rundown of all the software presently installed on your PC.
- From the "**All Programs**" tab, select **"Internet Explorer."** The default Internet browser that accompanies all Windows systems is Internet Explorer. Your machine will launch "Internet Explorer" once you select it, allowing you to start exploring the web.

Why is the Chrome Browser in My Windows 11 PC so Slow?

As you transition to Windows 11, you may notice that some websites and programs are slow and sluggish. Among the most typical causes is a problem with the hardware. It's possible that the application's performance will be slowed if you're using Windows 11 with poor hardware.

Experiment with different internet browsers and apps. If the problem remains, you might need to revert to an earlier edition of Windows. Nevertheless, given there are a few extreme cures you might attempt first, we recommend saving this remedy until last.

Browser Slowness in Windows 11 Troubleshooting

Clear Your Browser's Cache

The accumulation of website cache on internet browsers will cause some slowdowns in how fast is its speed. Cleaning the cache of your internet browser on a regular basis is suggested. Below is how you can clean Chrome's cache.

- Launch Google Chrome
- Launch the Menu and select Settings from the drop-down menu.
- On the left part of the screen, choose Privacy and Security.
- Choose Clear Browsing Data from the Privacy and Security menu.
- Decide on a time frame. Check that all of the other checkboxes are also checked.
- Select Clear Now from the menu.

Cookie Configurations

Cookies from reputable websites might help you have a better online experience. Contemplate permitting those from sites you visit if your default settings disable all cookies.

- Launch Google Chrome's menu and select Settings.

- Choose Cookies and some other website data from the Privacy and Security menu.

- Scroll downwards and select the Add tab beside "Sites that can always use cookies" under the Customized behaviors option.

- Type in the troublesome website URL, such as https://youtube.com or https://facebook.com. Then choose Add.

Turn off Synchronization

Background synchronization processes might consume a lot of network bandwidth. Hence, the user's internet connection is slowed. Every professional user can suspend synchronizations when surfing the web and resume them while not utilizing a computer.

- Enter "sync settings" into the Start Menu.

- Choose Sync your Settings from the menu.

- Turn off the Sync settings by clicking the switch button.

Optional Performance Changes

Windows 11 includes a number of effective tools for limiting your system's performance. This might have an impact on your network as well. If this is the situation, you might consider upgrading to a higher-performing system.

- Enter Performance of Windows into the Start Menu.
- Choose the option to change the performance and appearance of Windows.
- Choose Adjust for Best Performance from the Visual Effects tab.
- Select Apply and then OK.

Applications and Services in the Background Should be Turned off or Killed

Other programs, like Sync settings, could be active in the backdrop. This might include things like voice assistants, alerting services, and file indexers. It is preferable to have them turned off and just activate them when absolutely necessary.

- Enter Background applications into the Start Menu.

- Choose the programs that will run in the background.

- Switch off Allow applications to be active in the background in the Allow apps to run in the background section.

- To launch the Task Manager, hold down the Ctrl + Shift + Esc at the same time.

- Select More details.

- To arrange by use, select the Network option in Processes.

- Choose the undesired app you wish to delete.

- Select Finish Task from the menu.

- Rehash for each program that is consuming network resources.

Modify the Power Options

Windows 11 on laptops has a set of power choices. Windows 11 strives to operate the system with the least amount of power usage possible to extend battery capacity. Hence, even when connected, network performance might degrade.

- Go to the Start Menu, then search for "power plan."

- Choose a power plan from the drop-down menu.

- Select High-performance from the set of power options.

Restarting Network Adapter

In Windows 11, restarting the network adapter will reload the network settings. If there is a problem, a reboot would usually fix it.

- Enter network connections into the Start Menu.
- Choose View network connections from the drop-down menu.
- Right-click the network adapter symbol and choose Properties.
- Choose Disable.
- Wait a few seconds and then right-click once more.
- Click the Enable button.
- Wait for the adaptor to be activated again.

Verify DNS Configuration

It's possible that your computer's IP and DNS setups are incorrect. As a result, your internet connection will be sluggish or unavailable entirely. The best option for solutions is to change settings to receive settings from your router.

1. Go to the Start Menu and type Control Panel into the search box.

2. Choose Network and Internet from the menu.

3. Choose Network and Sharing Center from the menu.

4. Beside the Connections icon, hit on the existing connection.

5. Select Properties.

6. Choose Internet Protocol Version 4 from the menu.

7. Go to the Properties tab.

8. Double-check that the choices listed below are chosen.

9. Acquire an internet protocol automatically.

10. Get a DNS server address automatically

11. Click OK.

12. Select the Close button.

Drivers for Networking Should be updated

Your network device may also require a driver update after upgrading to Windows 11. Download the driver update following these procedures if the machine hasn't already done so.

1. Choose Device Manager from the Start Menu by right-clicking it.

2. To broaden the list, select Network adapters.

3. Right-click on the name of your computer's network adapter.

4. Click on the Update Driver.

5. Choose the option to search for drivers automatically.

6. If necessary, repeat for additional wireless or wired connections.

Disabling IPv6

IPv6 is the internet connection's sixth edition. As more access points are utilized throughout the globe, it is expected to become the internet's future norm. For the time being, all gadgets use and support IPv4, the present standard. To avoid any prospective network difficulties, IPv6 should be securely disabled in Windows 11.

1. Go to the Start Menu. Then type Control Panel into the search box.

2. Choose Network and Internet from the menu.

3. Choose Network and Sharing Center from the menu.

4. Beside the Connections icon, select the existing connections.

5. Select Properties.

6. Select TCP/IPv6 and uncheck it.

7. Select OK.

How to Search for Something

To seek help, programs, settings, files, and lots more, use the taskbar to search the internet and the Windows and the web. Also, you may use connections in the preview window to receive immediate solutions from the internet, such as currency conversion, stock prices, weather, and lots more.

For better accessibility to your favorite applications and current activity, simply tap or select Search. On the taskbar, click or touch Search, and enter what you are searching for in the text field to obtain query suggestions from the internet and your computer.

Pick a genre that fits your search goal to see additional outcomes of that sort: Web, Email, Documents, Apps, and lots more. You can choose a class either after or before you begin entering.

How to Open Videos

To watch a video on your computer, you'll need a video player that supports video files. If you've version 12 or higher of Windows Media Player, it'll play your video file, but if you've version 11 or lower, you'll need to deploy a codec or utilize a third-party media player like QuickTime or VLC.

Utilizing the Pre-installed Media Players

Get the video you want to play. Get a video file from a reputable website, a USB disk, or just access it from the PC's hard disk. It's critical that you understand what filename it's stored as and the location where it is stored. Choose the video from the File Browser by clicking File > Open.

Double-click it to activate it. Double-click the media player's icon to start seeing the video after you've found it in your OS (Operating System). The default video player will become active and show the video when you double-click it on the left-hand side of your mouse.

Windows Media Player will most probably be used to view the video. This in-built video player comes standard on all computers operating any edition of Windows. Without a third-party converter or codec, Windows 11 and below will have a hard time opening MP4 files.

Click the video using the right part of your mouse. If you're using the Windows operating system, rather than double-clicking on the video, you want to right-click on it to select the video player you want to utilize to watch your movie. A drop-down selection will appear as a result of this.

Select "Open With". A new cascading window will appear when you choose it within the drop-down list. A collection of different video players will appear on the screen. Windows Media Player and a host of other third-party video players that have been downloaded are most certainly among them.

Select Windows Media Player from the drop-down menu. Your preferred video will run in Windows if you've installed a decoder pack or code.

How to Make Registration on Sites?

Registering on sites is a very straightforward process that almost everyone can do. You'll be provided with forms that you should fill. Just add the relevant information and that will be it.

What Should You Do If You're Concerned About Internet Security?

A nineteen-year-old New Hampshire candidate running for a governmental position learned the hard way the necessity of adhering to online safety laws. His rivals discovered sexually provocative photographs and references to prior drug usage in his posts on social media, according to Seacoast Online. His career in politics had taken off and then collapsed and destroyed. Sadly, he isn't alone, as reckless online habits have subjected others to frauds, identity fraud, and physical violence from strangers they met on the internet. As more people utilize mobile gadgets to access the world wide web, these hazards are evolving and expanding at a rapid pace.

Despite the fact that applications are more prevalent in most individuals' everyday online communication than conventional media, the core online safety guidelines have not altered. Cybercriminals are still looking for private details that they may use to get control of their bank accounts and credit card details.

Also, insecure browsing can lead to additional dangers, such as humiliating personal remarks or photographs that are virtually hard to remove after they've been posted online, or becoming entangled with folks you don't want to associate with.

Keep Personal Details Limited and Professional

Your home address or personal life is not required information for prospective employers or consumers. They must be aware of your skills and professional experience, as well as how to contact you. You would not give out solely personal details to outsiders one-on-one, so why would you give it to every other person on the internet?

Make sure your privacy configurations are turned on.

Hackers and marketers both want to know everything about you. Your social media and browsing habits may teach both of these categories of people so much about you. However, you have control over your data. According to Lifehacker, both mobile OSes and browsers include privacy options that may be used to safeguard your digital security. Privacy-promoting features are also accessible on big platforms like Facebook. Corporations desire your private details for their advertising worth; thus, these preferences are often difficult to uncover. Ensure that you've got these privacy measures set and that you have them active.

Employ caution when browsing the internet.

You wouldn't go through a risky area, so don't go online and visit unsafe places. Lurid information is used as bait by hackers. They understand that consumers are occasionally enticed by questionable information and may relax their protection when looking for it. The demimonde of the world wide web is full of hidden dangers, where a single thoughtless click might reveal personal information or corrupt your computer with malware. You wouldn't even allow the cybercriminals an opportunity if you fight the desire.

Verify that Your Online Access is Safe

PCMag points out that when you browse the internet with a social internet facility, such as via a neighborhood Wi-Fi network, you've got no full control over your privacy. Endpoints—the locations where your private network interfaces to the world—are a source of concern for organizational cybersecurity specialists. Your personal internet connectivity is your susceptible endpoint. Check to see if your gadget is safe, and if you are not certain, wait till a good opportunity presents itself (i.e., when you can access a safe Wi-Fi connection) before entering sensitive details like your credit card details.

Use Caution When Downloading

Cybercriminals are mostly interested in tricking you into installing malware—applications or software that contain malware or attempt to steal your data. This virus may be camouflaged as an application, which might be anything from a famous game to a weather or transportation application. Downloading programs that appear questionable or originate from a source you don't know is not a good idea, according to PCWorld.

Use Secure Passwords

Passcodes are among the most vulnerable parts of the online security system, and there is presently no way to avoid them. And the trouble with these credentials is that individuals prefer to use simple-to-remember ones (like "1234" and "date of birth"), which are equally easy to deduce by cybercriminals. Choose complex passwords that really are difficult for attackers to crack. You may use password management software to keep track of several passwords to help you keep them handy and secure. A secure password is something that is both unique and complicated, consisting of at least fifteen characters that include special characters, numbers, and letters.

Use Secure Websites to Conduct Online Transactions

When you shop online, you must supply your bank account or credit card details, which is exactly what fraudsters want. Provide these details only to platforms that offer safe, secured connectivity. Secure websites may be identified by checking for a URL that begins with HTTPS instead of just HTTP, according to Boston University. A shutter symbol close to the URL space could also indicate them.

Be Wary of What You Share Online

As one inexperienced contender in New Hampshire discovered, the online world doesn't come with a delete button. Since deleting the source (like, from Twitter) doesn't erase any duplicates generated by others, any image or comment you upload on the internet may remain online indefinitely. You won't be able to "retrieve" a statement you regret making or delete that awkward picture you snapped at a gathering. Put nothing on the internet that you'd never like your mother or future boss to see.

Be Wary of Who You Encounter on the Internet

Individuals that you encounter on the internet aren't often who they say they are. It's possible that they're not even genuine. False social network identities are a common approach for hackers to snuggle up to naïve internet visitors and empty their online wallets, according to InfoWorld. Maintain the same level of caution and common sense in your online life that you do in your offline life.

Make sure Your Antivirus Software is Updated

Although Internet security software won't protect you from every attack, it will identify and delete the vast majority of malware—just make sure it's up to date. Make sure you're updated on your OS and any programs you're using. They add an important layer of protection.

If you follow these ten fundamental Internet safety guidelines, you'll be able to prevent several of the unpleasant shocks that lie on the web for the unwary.

Chapter 4: What are the Benefits of Windows 11?

The future of Windows has arrived, and guess what? It's causing quite a stir! The redesigned Windows has a plethora of options, from a dramatic overhaul to innovative functionalities that make your life simpler. There are several reasons to be thrilled about this new edition!

Windows enthusiasts could not be more enthusiastic about the new Windows 11. Since learning about the impending release of this new OS, a lot of techies have been actively evaluating hundreds of items to guarantee they're interoperable and easy to implement. So, what's all the commotion about?

What's the Huge Deal with Windows 11?

On October 5th, 2021, Microsoft officially released the latest edition of its operating system, and the hoopla surrounding Windows 11 has surpassed that of any prior Windows Operating system since the release of Windows 7. It was created to resemble the Linux and Mac OS environments.

The icons are now in the middle of the new taskbar. Those who don't like the centralized taskbar can change its appearance. Users may select the position they want the Start button, applications, and icons to be.

In addition, the new Windows offers a superior gameplay experience. It allows game players access to some of the greatest Xbox capabilities. Given that Xbox is one of Microsoft's products, it's only natural that the most recent edition of Windows incorporates Xbox functionality for Computer gamers.

Other things that consumers have been looking forward to are:

- A more unified user interface
- Enhanced multi-monitor functionality
- A solitary monitor with many desktops
- Transparent Windows
- Improved interactivity with touchscreens
- The launch of the Microsoft Store

Let's take a look at a few of the primary advantages of Windows 11 now that we have gone through the various features associated with the newest Microsoft operating system.

Windows 11's Seven Most Valuable Features

Consumers have either liked their operating system for over a decade or they've been waiting for the arrival of a superior edition, such as those who are still using Windows 7. Consumers are eager to see if Windows 11 will live up to the promise, with lots of flexibility and simple integration.

The glorious times of Windows 98 SE are still remembered by critics. Microsoft, on the other hand, is convinced that they have created an environment that all computer users would appreciate. Here are the features that Microsoft claims render Windows 11 their finest OS to date:

AI-Driven Widgets

Widgets have made a comeback! If you like widgets (the hovering informative windows featured on Vista and Windows) to the Live Tiles featured on Windows 10, you're going to be a satisfied user.

The Windows 11 redesigned widgets are better integrated with the operating system and feature a more user-friendly design. The dedicated pane pulls out from the left-hand part of your display, allowing you to locate what you're looking for without having to navigate through the rest of the screen.

Android Applications

For Android applications, Windows 11 includes an in-built marketplace. The giant tech company launched Microsoft Store, which allows you to get content without having to journey down to Google Play Store.

While some Windows fans have always been able to run Android applications using their Windows 10 computer, this is the very first time that everyone will be able to do just that.

However, certain programs that are available on the Play Store will not be available on Microsoft Store. Users will, nevertheless, be successful in obtaining:

- TikTok
- Disney Plus
- Pinterest
- Netflix
- Uber

Virtual Desktops

Isolated virtual desktops can be created in Windows 11. You may personalize them with various backgrounds to help you manage and recognize them. These virtual workspaces are more akin to that manner that the Mac OS uses in switching between programs or applications on your system screen.

Microsoft Team

Users of Windows 11 may now incorporate their videoconferencing service, Teams, with this update. Users may join using a variety of devices and platforms, like Windows 10 laptops and desktops, Xbox gaming systems, and Apple's iOS devices. You can effortlessly do this while staying in touch with your coworkers, family, and friends from anywhere on the planet.

Snap Layouts

What if it is possible to have infinite windows open at the same time on your computer monitor? Think about having the ability to see everything that is going on around and in front of you while you are working in your workspace. This is achievable thanks to a new capability in Windows 11.

Snap Layouts allows you to combine many layouts on a single screen. You may also store those window designs in the order you want them.

When you launch a new window, there is always an opportunity to configure that screen in the upper right-hand corner. Pick your chosen design from the possible options by clicking on the box close to the X.

Snap Groups

A snap group is a collection of active windows that have been preserved in Snap Layouts. They're simply accessible and may be located in your system's taskbar. You may then reduce or increase their size as a bunch. Whenever you want them, the different groups you made will appear. All you've got to do now is select the one you want and the whole group will reopen.

How to Turn Off/On Windows 11 Notifications

The alert system in Windows 11 differs somewhat from that of earlier Windows editions. Those who used to switch off alerts in previous operating system editions would most probably do so with Windows 11.

Enabling or Disabling Alerts on Windows 11

We have your back if you like the tranquility that comes with disabling alerts for particular applications or on the core level.

This section will teach you what you can do to re-enable or switch off alerts for all applications or just a few of them. On Windows 11 PCs, there are a few distinct methods to achieve this:

- In the Settings option, you may deactivate or allow alerts at the core level.

- In the Settings option, you may block or allow alerts exclusively for particular applications.

- Using the Registry Editor, you may deactivate or enable Notifications at the System level.

- Using the Notification Center, you may block or allow alerts for certain senders or applications.

We've addressed every possible option, so choose from any option you feel more comfortable with based on how you'd like to change the behavior of alerts you'd be receiving in Windows 11.

All Windows 11 alerts may be turned off or on from the Settings menu.

- On Windows 11, hit the Windows button + I to enter the Settings option.

- From the default Settings page, select System from the left-hand menu. Hit the action icon on the upper left-hand side of your screen if you have a problem seeing the default options.

- Now that you are in the System section, go to the right menu and choose Notifications.

- Finally, under the menu of the dedicated Notifications, flip the switch to OFF to turn off all alerts from all applications, or ON if you'd like to get all alerts.

- The latest behavior is what will be imposed the moment you adjust the toggle. At this time, you can securely exit the Settings page.

Certain Windows alerts can be turned off or on using the Settings option. This is how to do it:

- To access the Settings screen, hit Windows key + I.

- Select System from the left-hand vertical option by clicking or tapping on it.

Note: If this option isn't accessible by design, go to the upper right-hand corner of the display and hit the action button. Select the System tab and then click or touch on Notifications on the right side of the window.

1. Scroll downwards and locate the notifications from other senders and applications areas of the Notifications settings section and switch on or off the specific switch for the applications you wish to get alerts from.

2. You can freely exit the Settings page after the modifications have been applied.

Using the Registry Editor to switch off or on all Windows 11 Alerts

1. To launch the Run dialog box, hold down the Windows key + R. To launch a Registry Editor window with administrator access, input the term 'Regedit' into the text field that just opened, then hit Ctrl + Shift + Enter. Launch the Registry Editor program.

2. When the User Account Control warning appears, select Yes to provide administrator access.

3. Once within the Registry Editor, browse to the subsequent area using the option on the Windows left corner:

HKEY_CURRENT_USER\Software\Microsoft\Windows\CurrentVersion\PushNotifications

---

Keep in Mind: You may either physically browse to this page or put the address into the space at the head of the Registry Editor and hit Enter to go there right away.

---

4. From the left-hand menu, right-click the Push Notifications option and select New > Dword Value from the action menu that appears. Make a fresh Dword.

5. Then, check out the right-hand pane and right-click on the Dword that you recently created, and select Rename. Change the title of the recent Dword that you recently created.

6. Double-click on the Toast Enabled object that you recently created, then change the value to 1 and Hexadecimal 1 according to your needs:

7. Deactivate the alerts at a root level on Windows 11

8. Activate the alerts at a root level on Windows 11

9. After making the modification, quit the Registry Editor and restart your computer to have the modifications materialize.

You Can Turn Off Alerts on Windows from the Notification Center

Keep in Mind: You can only employ this approach if you have a notice from the application, you're trying to change the default alert behavior for.

1. Hit Windows key + N to launch the Notification Center.

2. Then, go to the head of the application and select the three-dotted icon (action button) to shut off alerts.

3. Select Turn off all alerts for *application name* from the menu bar that just displayed.

4. Quit the Settings application because the modifications should have taken effect already.

Hotkeys: What Are They and How Do You Use Them?

Hotkeys are keyboard keys that perform a function when pressed alone or in conjunction with some other keys. Hotkeys allow quick access to common actions that might otherwise require menu browsing. Utilizing macros to generate hotkey functionalities, users may set commands to keys inside numerous software packages.

Most OSes come with a set of in-built hotkeys, most of which have been standardized to aid users who may transfer operating systems or utilize many platforms. Conventional hotkeys are included in software applications such as browsers, spreadsheets, and word processors, aside from customized hotkeys particular to the application.

Pressing the control key while hitting the C key copies highlighted content to the clipboard on Windows operating systems. Ctrl + V captures the text and pastes it into an open window. To cut the text, press Ctrl + X, and to undo an action, press Ctrl + Z. F1 is the typical key to Help menus, while the F-keys are widely utilized by themselves.

User-programmable additional buttons are available on certain keyboards. Custom hotkeys can be created by assigning macros to these additional keys. Customized hotkeys are very helpful in productivity apps, debugging apps, and gaming apps.

The 'Fn' or 'Ctrl' keys are commonly used as hotkeys.

It's simple to program a hotkey. The procedure usually takes seconds and entails starting a macro script to capture the steps needed to perform the desired operation. The captured actions are allocated to the button as if they were a script (s). From that moment on, clicking the hotkey will start the process, repeating the operation. The macro application, for instance, maybe found under Tools > Macro > Record New Macro in Microsoft Word.

Consult the basic Help menu for a list of available hotkeys available in your system. Look up "hotkeys" or "keyboard shortcuts" on the internet. Copying the listing and having it on hand might help you remember the hotkeys you use the most. Check within your preferred software products, such as your email app, productivity apps, and internet browser, too.

Utilizing hotkeys can boost productivity while also reducing repeated mouse motions that can lead to carpal tunnel disease. Seriously look for a hotkey combo or make yours if you notice yourself grabbing your mouse often to perform an essential function or task all the time.

Hotkey shortcuts can lessen the chance of developing carpal tunnel sickness and a host of other wrist ailments caused by repetitive usage.

How to Connect to a Network in Windows 11

What You Should Know

- Open the action center from the taskbar and follow this route: Manage Wi-Fi Connections > Connect to (name of the network).

- Click Network & internet > Wi-Fi > Show Available Networks > Show Available Networks> (network name) > Connect from the Windows Settings.

- Select Network and Internet > Connect to the Internet > (network name) > Connect from device's Control Panel.

How To Connect Your Windows Computer to Any Network?

If your PC includes an Ethernet connection, you can get it connected to a network through an Ethernet connection, or you may use Wi-Fi if that's not feasible. The control panel, Windows Settings, and the taskbar are the three options for connecting a Windows 11 PC to a Wi-Fi network. Each way achieves the same goal, so choose the one that is most comfortable for you.

How to Get Connected to a Wi-Fi in Your Windows 11 PC from the Taskbar

The taskbar is generally the quickest way of connecting to a Wi-Fi connection. A number of important features have shortcuts on the taskbar. If your PC's taskbar has not been altered, you'll see these controls on its right-hand side, close to the time and date. Pressing the power sound, or network icon in Windows 11 brings up the Quick Settings option, where you may access a network.

Ignore this part and attempt the approach mentioned in the following step if you didn't locate the network or Wi-Fi options on your PC's taskbar.

In Windows 11, you can connect your PC to a Wi-fi connection via the taskbar like this:

1. To access the Quick Settings page, hit the Action Center symbol on the taskbar (power, sound, and network icons to the left-hand side of the date and time option).

2. On your PC's Quick Settings page, select Manage Wi-Fi Connections in the upper left-hand corner of your PC.

3. Select a Wi-Fi network to connect to.

4. If the Wi-Fi icon on your PC is now disabled, you must first hit the Wi-Fi switch.

5. Press the Connect button.

6. Input your Wi-Fi password when required, then click Next.

7. The Wi-Fi connection will be established on your PC.

How to Use Windows Settings to Join a Wi-Fi Connection

If the Action Center and Quick Settings menus aren't working for you, you may use Windows Settings to connect to a Wi-Fi network.

Below is how you can use Windows Settings to access a network:

1. On your taskbar, have the Stat button right-clicked and select Settings.

2. Select Network and Internet from the drop-down menu.

3. If the Wi-Fi switch is turned off, click it.

4. Select Wi-Fi.

5. Select Show Available Networks from the drop-down menu.

6. From the options, select a Wi-Fi network.

7. Choose Connect, and if required, provide the password to the network.

8. Your computer will establish a network connection.

How to Use the Control Panel in Windows 11 to Look for Wi-Fi Networks

The Settings panel in Windows 11 now contains the majority of the features formerly present in the Control Panel of prior editions of Windows. If you want, you might access a network through the Control Panel, but this requires a few more processes and effectively evokes the very same network option that can be reached straight from the Quick Settings button on the taskbar.

From the control panel in Windows 11, follow these steps to access a connection:

1. On your taskbar, hit the search symbol (this looks like a magnifying lens).

2. Enter the term "control panel" into the search area.

3. In your search results, choose Control Panel.

4. Select Network and Internet from the drop-down menu.

5. Select Connect to the Internet from the drop-down menu.

6. If Wi-Fi is turned off, hit the Wi-Fi switch to switch it on.

7. Select a Wi-Fi connection to connect to.

8. Press Connect, and if required, provide the password to the network.

9. Your machine will join the network of your choice.

When Your Windows 11 PC Cannot Establish a Connection, What Should You Do?

There are very few things that are more aggravating than a PC that refuses to establish a connection. This section of this book will show you exactly what to do when your PC refuses to make that connection.

Why am I unable to join a network?

Since there are many vulnerabilities in wireless connections, they are complicated. Identifying the source of a connectivity problem can be tricky, ranging from the Wi-Fi toggle to a programming problem, router problem, or ISP issue.

Poorly configured parameters and geographical barriers from the connection source are among the two major reasons why your Windows PC will find it hard to establish that connection. However, there are more possibilities: Wi-Fi is off, a package of malware has disrupted the connectivity, the network needs special authorization, or the connection is overloaded.

How Can I Solve Connectivity Issues?

Follow these steps in order, checking following each of the steps to determine whether the issue has been remedied, considering all the probable causes for connectivity troubles with Windows 11.

Double-check that it's a Windows 11 issue

When it affects other endpoints on the connection, there is no need to treat it as though you are solving a system problem.

If your smartphone, smart speakers, some other PCs, and other devices can all access the web regularly, you may reasonably imagine the problem is with the Windows 11 computer and proceed with these procedures.

Also, this is a great opportunity to check if the issue is limited to one webpage or affects your entire machine. If you can access Twitter,

YouTube, or Google from the computer, but your company's website is finding it hard to load, the issue is with that specific site, has nothing to do with your machine or connection. Your only true alternatives are to email that website or to wait for the issue to be resolved.

Shut down and restart your device

Restarting is a standard troubleshooting procedure for most electrical devices, and it may be everything that is required to resolve your Windows 11 connection issues.

Restarting from your desktop is as simple as right-clicking the Start option and selecting sign out > Restart or Shut down.

Check that Wi-Fi is switched on or off that the Ethernet wire between the machine and the router/modem is properly connected

This is critical, and if it's not resolved, you won't be able to connect to the internet.

To activate Wi-Fi, certain computers feature a tangible switch that must be switched. Others utilize FN+F2 or FN+F5 as a hotkey combo. Also, Wi-Fi switches can be accessed in this route: Settings > Network & Internet > Wi-Fi.

Remove and afterward re-include the Wi-Fi connection

This will restart the connectivity from scratch, comparable to resetting your computer. It's possible that there was a problem with the manner the Wi-Fi data was stored the initial time it was inputted on your PC, or that a component of your PC damaged the data. this gives you the chance to re-input your password or SSID if you entered them wrongly in the first place.

Go to the Settings page and locate Network & Internet > Wi-Fi > Manage recognized networks > Add a new network to re-create the connectivity.

If you are utilizing Wi-Fi, get nearer to the gadget that's giving the internet connectivity

A network's range is limited, and some endpoints are unable to receive a transmission from a distant location.

The simplest method to reduce proximity as a factor for your inability to connect to the internet is to move nearer to the base station or move it nearer to you.

If you have determined that this is the issue but can't move your access point or computer, upgrade to one that can transmit the signal farther and attach an auxiliary wireless network device to your PC.

Physically select the Wi-Fi connection

Even if you're near enough and have everything established perfectly, if your Windows 11 PC is not informed to create a connection, it could be a connectivity problem.

To access Wi-Fi, go over to Network & Internet > Wi-Fi > To locate a Wi-Fi connection, display all accessible connections. Choose it, then click Connect automatically > Connect.

Launch a browser and continue with the on-screen instructions to access the network.

In most circumstances, this is necessary after selecting an open Wi-Fi connection. This will not be seen on other networks, such as your house network.

You may need to double-check your credentials on that screen, which normally includes your name and email address, but may also include additional data such as your hotel suite number if you are staying there. You may have to pay a subscription in some instances, such as aboard an airline.

Switch off any other connection-related technologies that may be conflicting with Windows' right to access the connection for the time being.

Some instances are as follows:

- Turn off Airplane Mode
- Exit your VPN server.

- Turn off your device's firewall and put the antivirus program on hold.

- Disable the 'metered connection' option.

Make sure your network driver is up to date.

If a new update tempered with it, it might have to be upgraded or restored to the prior driver.

The simplest method for updating your driver is to have it installed from a machine with active internet connectivity and then transfer it to the Windows 11 machine. By winding back your driver, you can reverse an update that was recently made.

Certain driver updating programs allow you to search your machine for absent or obsolete drivers before downloading them from a computer with working network connectivity. It makes determining the proper driver a breeze.

1. Make sure Windows is up to date. If a recently made driver update did not solve it or an upgrade wasn't required, Windows Update may have a connection-related issue patch.

2. Utilize the in-built Windows connection troubleshooter to diagnose and resolve network issues. Go to Settings > Network & Internet > Network troubleshooter to get you there.

3. Go to Settings > Network & Internet > Network reset > Reset now to refresh the network configuration. This will go ahead and reinstall your access points and restore the default configuration of essential network elements.

It's possible that there is nothing that you could do. This was mentioned in the first step. In several circumstances, a gadget's inability to establish a Wi-Fi connection is only a symptom of a larger issue beyond your reach.

If you are utilizing your neighborhood connection, such as one at a restaurant or a hotel, it's conceivable that there are just too many individuals online at the same time. Because bandwidth is really not infinite, a limit of the gadgets will be exceeded at a certain time, and based on whatever they are trying to accomplish online (e.g., streaming or downloading), it may be achieved earlier than normal. There isn't much you could do right from your system to help you if you are facing this.

Some problems can be traced back to your Internet service provider or the network equipment you're utilizing. If, for instance, your entire district is without internet, it's evident that following the procedures above will not help you get connected.

Likewise, your connection point may be obsolete or failing, which is simpler to see if you've got many gadgets trying to access. If this is the case, you can consider upgrading your router, switching to a better one, or restarting the router.

Chapter 5: How to Adjust Display Scale Settings in Windows 11

You should probably modify the scale settings if items are too tiny and the text is difficult to read. While Windows 11 may automatically arrange display scaling configurations to ensure that items (navigations, icons, text, and lots more) are readable and the correct size, it isn't flawless, and manual adjustments might well be required sometimes.

If you don't have excellent eyesight, for example, enlarging the components on the larger display may make things simpler to see and operate while reducing eye strain. If you attach an extra monitor, you may use a customized scale option to make the menus, icons, and text larger on all of the displays. Adjusting the size of Windows 11 also may enhance the seeing of the computer while using a projector to display a presentation.

We'll show you how to modify the scale preferences on a laptop display or desktop monitor in this section. Follow these instructions to adjust the screen scale dimensions in Windows 11 with these recommended configurations:

1. Go to the Settings menu.

2. Select System.

3. On the right side, click the Display page button.

4. Choose the scale option from the Scale drop-down box in the "Scale & layout" area — for instance, 100 percent, 125 percent, 150 percent, or 175 percent.

The new display resolution will take effect once you've completed the instructions. While it's not necessary, you might have to reboot your PC to ensure that the changes take effect.

How to Adjust the Display Size in Windows 11 Using Custom Settings?

Custom values should not be used to adjust the scale parameters since it impacts the visual experience. Nevertheless, if it is required and carried out appropriately, it may be sufficient.

Follow these procedures to establish a custom scale dimension for your screen:

title

1. Go to the Settings menu.

2. Select System.

3. On the right-hand side, press the Display tab button.

4. Choose the Scale configuration from the "Scale & layout" tab.

5. Select a custom scaling level between one hundred and five hundred percent in the "Custom scaling" tab.

Fast Hint: If you wish to increase the app or text size, set the value to be around one hundred and ten percent.

---

1. Select Check from the menu.

2. Select "Sign out now" from the menu.

3. Log in to your account again.

Your PC will apply the modification you chose when you finish the procedures. If your PC isn't scaling items appropriately, carry out the steps once more to choose another value to raise or reduce the scaling value till you reach the desired result.

You may always undo your adjustments by following the same steps as before, but at step 4, select the Turn off customized scaling and log out option.

How to Create Bigger Texts Without Altering the Scale Configurations on Your Windows 11 PC

You shouldn't change the scale parameters if you'd like to create more readable texts. Rather, with Windows 11, you should just change the font size options. Follow these procedures to produce larger texts on your desktop:

1. Go to the Settings menu.
2. Select Accessibility from the menu.
3. On the right-hand side, select the Text size tab.
4. To increase the font size in Windows 11, utilize the "Text size" slider.
5. Select "Apply" from the menu.

The display will show a "Please wait" notice once you've completed the instructions, and the new font size will be applied.

How Can I Enjoy a 1920x1080 Pixel Density on Windows 11?

If your machine does not automatically default to the 1080P quality in Windows 11, it means that you may manually alter the option. True, before you could even alter the quality, your display must support it. A screen that only allows a quality of 720P (1280x720), for instance, wouldn't operate at 1920x1080 since it lacks the necessary resolution. To adjust the quality to 1920x1080, open the screen configuration and follow the instructions below.

1. On your system taskbar, hit on the Windows symbol

2. Find and choose the Settings application symbol.

3. Select Display to get the display options.

4. Browse down to the Scale & Layout section.

5. To agree to the modifications, choose the 1920x1080 screen quality from the right-hand drop-down option.

How Can I Enjoy a 1920x1080 Display Quality on a 1366x768 Display?

You can't update to the 1920x1080 display quality if you are using a monitor that automatically adjusts the quality to 1366x768, for example.

The explanation for this is that the monitor you're using doesn't support the 1920x1080 display quality. Even though you go out of your way and utilize third-party programs to adjust the display quality, like Custom Resolution Utility, owing to the down-sampling required to display objects at that pixel density on a display that does not allow it, some text and some other things might be illegible.

It's also worth noting that several third-party programs that enable you to select custom resolution choices might not be completely supported until Windows 11 is officially released.

How to Make Icons and Text Larger Without Adjusting Your Resolution

Also, you can scale your screen down or up to modify the dimension of icons and texts without changing the quality. When you scale up, the icons and text look larger, and when you scale down, they appear smaller.

To alter your screen's scaling factor, go to the Settings application from the Start Menu's pinned applications or by entering it in the Windows search space. Then, ensure that the 'System' option is chosen from the window's left sidebar. Then, on the right side of your device's Settings page, select the 'Display' button. Browse down to and locate the 'Scale

& layout' area and select the 'Scale' tile to display specific scaling options.

Then, based on your specific use application, you can specify a figure. Your display's scaling factor is set to one hundred percent by convention. Input a value of more than one hundred to make your device's icons and text larger; alternatively, input a number that is lower than one hundred and select the 'check mark' positioned directly next to the text field to render the text tinier. Only once you logged out/reboot your system will the scale factor be applied.

> **Note**: Ensure you're not severely adjusting the scaling multiplier and instead give it a modest decrease/increase, since a drastic drop or increase may make the display exceedingly hard to navigate.

The chosen scale factor will enter into force after you login back in.

That's all there is to it; these are the many methods you may change your pixel density or/and make icons and text smaller or larger to suit your needs.

What Should I Do When My Screen Settings Are Invalid?

You may adjust your screen resolution on your personal computer by following these steps: To access the Personalization screen, right-click an empty space on the desktop and select "Personalize." At the end of the list, select "Display Settings." Press, hold and drag the bar in "Resolution" to change the resolution. The original quality of your display is the maximum possible resolution.

Why Can I Not Alter the Resolution of My Display?

The most common cause of this problem is driver failure. When drivers aren't interoperable, they default to a lower display resolution to be safe. So, let's start by updating your graphics drivers or reverting to an earlier version.

Why Can I not Resize My Taskbar or Start Menu in Windows 11?

You won't be able to adjust the taskbar or Start menu in Windows 11's first retail launch in October 2021, as many users could with Windows 10. We understand your annoyance and are trying to figure out some possible solutions.

Windows 11: A Partially Complete, Lent Heritage from Windows 10X

The Windows operating system is based on Windows 10X, which was created by the giant tech company for a unique type of hardware framework with two displays. The Start Menu and taskbar were modified along the way to make them more user-friendly. Microsoft adopted the Windows 10X to single-display gadgets after ditching the dual-display idea, and later moved Windows 10X interface components (like a revamped taskbar or Start menu) to Windows 11.

We were glued with a significantly streamlined taskbar and Start menu when Windows 11 launched sometime in October 2021. You cannot adjust the taskbar or Start menu, for instance, and you cannot move the taskbar about the display. (Fortunately, you can relocate the Start menu to the taskbar's left-hand side.)

It's conceivable that Microsoft may add these functions to Windows 11 in their looming patches—and we pray it does. Microsoft will most probably keep improving Windows 11 as time goes on. It's unclear if Microsoft deems a scalable Start menu or taskbar to be an advancement.

Start Menu and Taskbar Solutions

In Windows 11, you can relocate the items on your taskbar to your screen's left-hand side (such as the Start button), but you cannot adjust the taskbar directly. There's a fix that entails altering the Windows Registry, only that it comes with significant drawbacks: The outcomes aren't ideal, and there are just three sizes available.

We do not really know any way of resizing the Start menu on your PC, but you may theoretically revamp it. Stardock has built an application known as Start11 that lets you change the Start menu in your Windows 11 PC to one that looks more like Windows 10. Furthermore, a freeware Start substitute known as Open-Shell has been reported to run on Windows 11 with a few changes. Open-developers Shell is planning to introduce complete Windows 11 functionality in the future.

In the absence of those options, the right approach may be to mail Microsoft feedback via its feedback application known as Feedback Hub that is featured in Windows 11. To achieve this, go to Start and type "feedback," then select the Feedback Hub app icon from the results.

Select "Suggest a Feature" when the session starts, then enter in the specifics of what you want to see.

You may also use social networking sites to shoot messages to Microsoft (like Twitter). But try to be courteous—Microsoft programmers are working hard to create the greatest product possible, even though we do not often approve of design decisions. In the times ahead, there'll often be room for flexibility.

Shortcuts for Windows 11

Microsoft introduces fascinating fresh keyboard shortcuts to each new edition of Windows to increase productivity and efficiency for average users. Quick Settings, Action Center, Layouts, and Widgets are just a few of the recent keyboard shortcuts in Windows 11, which you could find quite helpful. Let's examine them in further depth.

Click on Win + A Shortcut in the Action Center.

Although the Win + A shortcut is technically accessible in Windows 10, it differs significantly in Windows 11. This key combination launches the Notification Panel and Control Center in Windows 10. However, with Windows 11, the Action Center and the Quick Settings window are the only things that appear. Since Microsoft's current desktop operating system splits the Notification Panel and Control Center, this is the case.

Press Win + N to Launch Notifications Panel

Windows 11 introduces the Win + N shortcut. It launches the Notification Panel that is presently buried in your device's System tray behind the clock symbol. All of your unopened alerts will be displayed if you use this hotkey.

Press Win + W to Launch Widgets Panel

A separate widgets pane in Windows 11 gives you easy accessibility to the calendar, news, and weather. While Windows 11 has a specific Widgets panel option on its taskbar, it is also possible to use the Win key + W hotkey to access it.

Press Win + Z Shortcut for Easy Accessibility to Snap Layout

Snap Layouts is a major update in Windows 11 that builds upon Windows 10's Snap window organization. When you mouse through the "Maximize" icon on any current session, it shows a pop-up with various Snap window configurations. This function is known as "Snap Assist" by Microsoft, and you may use the Win + Z hotkey to use it.

Keyboard Shortcuts in Windows 11

To make it easier for you to recall and utilize the current hotkeys, we've divided them into eleven sections. In Windows, you may find numerous hotkeys in the groups mentioned below:

1. Common keyboard shortcuts
2. Shortcuts for taking screenshots
3. Shortcuts in your web browser
4. Shortcuts in the dialog box
5. Shortcuts for accessibility
6. Shortcuts for the command prompt
7. Shortcuts for file explorer
8. Taskbar shortcuts
9. Shortcuts for game bar
10. Virtual desktop and desktop hotkeys, and lots more.

Common Shortcuts

The following are the Windows 11 hotkeys that everyone ought to know in order to have a more effective workflow and improve efficiency. They perform with the vast majority of applications, in the vast majority of circumstances, and in all latest Windows versions.

> **Remember**: Certain hotkeys in this section have several headings because they function in various applications in various instances. Depending on the requirement of the software or app class, they may work a bit differently in some instances.

- Press Alt + F4 to close any current window. This shortcut launches the exit dialog box with choices to shut down, log out, hibernate, sleep, or restart your computer while you're on the workstation with no current window active.

- Lock your computer by pressing the Win + L keys together.

- Press Win + D to close all current windows and return to your desktop.

- Switch between open applications by pressing Alt + Tab

- Launch Task View by pressing Win + Tab

- Undo an operation using Ctrl + Z.

- Redo an activity with Ctrl + Y.

- Delete + Ctrl: Toss the item in the recycle bin that you've chosen:

- Shift + Delete: Completely removes the chosen item.
- Press Win + X to access the context menu for the Start Button.
- Esc: Terminate or dismiss an active task
- F11: Exit/Enter the Full-screen mode
- Press the F2 key to rename the item you've chosen.
- Press F5 to reload the current window. When no current window is chosen, this shortcut reloads the desktop as well.
- Press F10 to access the present application's menu bar.
- Press Win + I to access the Windows 11 Options menu.
- Access the Run command by pressing Win + R.
- Move up a display using Alt + Page Up.
- Move down a display by pressing Alt + Page Down.
- In Windows 11, the hotkey Ctrl + Shift + Esc opens Task Manager.
- Launch Windows Search by pressing Win + Q or Win + S.
- Print a page using Ctrl + P.
- Select multiple items with Shift + Arrow keys

- Save an existing file by pressing Ctrl + S. (function on applications such as Paint, Notepad, Office 365, etc.)

- Save As (Ctrl+ Shift+ S)

- Press Ctrl + O to access files in the currently open application.

- Press Alt + Esc to loop through taskbar applications.

- On login pages, pressing Alt + F8 will show your password.

- Press Alt + Spacebar to bring up the present window's shortcut menu.

- Press Alt + Enter to access an item's attributes.

- Press Alt + F10 to access the chosen item's menu.

- Press Ctrl + N to access a fresh program window for the current application.

- Backspace: Return to the home page of Settings

- Open the Emoji selections in Windows 11 by pressing Win + period or Win + semicolon.

- Project a display by pressing Win + P.

- Start Voice Typing by pressing Win + H.

Shortcuts for Screenshots

The following section of this book will teach you how you can capture screenshots in Windows 11 as well as how you can capture scrolling screenshots, but below are some of the most used native screenshot hotkeys in Windows 11:

- Take a snapshot of the complete desktop with Print Screen/PrtScn.

- Take a snapshot of the current Window by pressing Alt + PrtScn.

- With Snip & Sketch, press Win + Shift + S to capture any section of the screen.

Shortcuts for Text Editor and Dialog Box

The majority of the hotkeys listed here function with all text boxes and dialog boxes, be it on your computer or the web. This includes internet forms, content management systems like WordPress, MS Word, Wordpad, and notepad. Some of them, however, are only available in some special text editors and will not function in programs such as Notepad.

- Select all material with Ctrl + A.

- Press Ctrl + C to copy the things you've selected.

- Press Ctrl + X to cut the things you've selected.

- Press Ctrl + V to paste the contents from the clipboard.

- Press Ctrl + B to bolden the highlighted text

- Italicize texts with Ctrl + I

- Press Ctrl + U to underline the text you want to highlight

- Home: Place your cursor at the beginning of the present line.

- Go to the present line's end using the pointer.

Browser Hotkeys

All popular Windows browsers such as Opera, Microsoft Edge, Mozilla Firefox, and Google Chrome, support the shortcuts below. In Windows 11, you can effortlessly change the default browser without bothering about keyboard shortcut compliance. These are some of the popular browser hotkeys in Windows 11.

- Press Alt + Left Arrow to return one page

- Press Alt + Right Arrow to advance one page.

- Tab Switching with Ctrl + Numbers (1-9)

- Ctrl + Tab will take you to the right-hand tab.

- Ctrl + Shift + Tab will take you to the leftmost tab.

- Press Ctrl + F to launch an on-page inquiry (functions on command prompt, word processors, text editors, etc.)

- Shift + Home will highlight text by moving the pointer to the beginning of the present line.

- Shift + End will highlight text by moving the pointer to the preset line's end.

- Shift Left/Right Arrow Keys will help you highlight/select a single character per time.

All of the above-mentioned dialog box actions, as well as most of the more generic ones, such as Alt+F4 to dismiss windows, function in browsers. However, the tab shortcuts function in some other tabbed programs, such as Windows Terminal.

Shortcuts for Virtual Desktop and Desktops

- Press the Windows key to access the Start Menu.

- Press Ctrl + Shift to change the keyboard appearance.

- Use Alt + Tab to see all active applications.

- Select multiple items on your desktop using Ctrl + Arrow keys + Spacebar.

- Press Win + M to close all active windows.

- Press Win + Shift + M to maximize all the windows that have been minimized.

- Press Win + Home to maximize or minimize all windows except the running one.

- Left Arrow Key + Win will Move the current window or app to the left-hand side.

- Winning + Correct Snap the present window or application to the right-hand side using the arrow buttons.

- Extend the current window to the bottom and top of your display by pressing Win + Shift + Up arrow button.

- Vertically restore or reduce current desktop windows while keeping width by pressing Win + Shift + down arrow buttons.

- Launch the Desktop mode by pressing Win + Tab.

- Add an additional virtual desktop by pressing Win + Ctrl + D.

- Quit the current virtual desktop by pressing Win + Ctrl + F4.

- Win + Ctrl + Right Arrow will change to virtual desktops towards the right.

- Switch to the virtual desktops on the left by pressing Win + Ctrl + Left Arrow.

- Create a shortcut with Ctrl + Shift

- Windows Peek (Win + Comma

- In Windows 11, press Win + Ctrl + Shift + B to restart your graphics driver immediately.

Command Prompt Shortcuts

The basic text editing actions for copying, pasting, and modifying commands are supported by the Terminal, Windows PowerShell, and Command Prompt. they support the specialized keyboard shortcuts listed below:

- Press Ctrl + Home to open the Command Prompt interface and scroll all the way to the top.

- Press Ctrl + End to scroll down to the command prompt window's base with Ctrl + End.

- Press Ctrl + A to select all items on the present line.

- Go up a page using the pointer.

- Go down a page using the pointer.

- Press Ctrl + M to go into the "Mark" view.

- Press Ctrl + Home to move your pointer to the start of the buffer in mark mode.

- Ctrl + End to move your pointer to the end of the buffer in mark mode.

- Move up and down with the arrow keys, and go through the present session's command history.

- Move the pointer right or left on the present command line using the right/left arrow button.

- Pressing Shift + Home will place the pointer to the beginning of the present line.

- Shift + End: This will take you to a present line's end with the cursor.

- Shift + Page Up: This will highlight text by moving the pointer up a screen.

- Shift + Page Down: Will select text by moving the pointer down a screen.

- Move a screen up one line by pressing Ctrl + Up arrow.

- Move a screen down one line with Ctrl + Down arrow.

- Shift + Up arrow: Will highlight text by moving the pointer up a line.

- Shift + Down arrow: Will highlight text by moving the pointer down a line.

- Ctrl + Shift + Arrow Keys will move the pointer a word per time with the keys.

Shortcuts in the File Explorer

The File Explorer includes its own hotkeys for traversing the Windows file module. Below is a list of the approximately twenty-four Windows File Explorer shortcuts:

- Press Win + E to launch the File Explorer

- Choose Search in your File Explorer by pressing Ctrl + E or Ctrl + F.

- Press Ctrl + N to launch a new window with the present page.

- Press Ctrl + W to close a running window.

- Change the folder and file display by pressing Ctrl + Mouse Scroll (shift between detailed view, list, large icons, small icons, etc.)

- Changes the folder view by pressing Ctrl + Shift + Number (1-8)

- Press F6 to toggle between the right and left panels.

- Create a fresh folder by pressing Ctrl + Shift + N.

- Press Ctrl + Shift + E to open all subdirectories in the left-hand navigation window.

- Choose the address bar in the File Explorer by pressing Alt + D.

- Press Alt + P to bring up the preview window.

- Press Alt + Enter to see the item's Properties options.

- Visit the subsequent folder by pressing Alt + Right arrow.

- Press Alt + Left arrow) to return to the previous directory.

- Press Alt + Up arrow to go to the current file/parent folder's folder.

- F4: Move the attention to the address bar.

- Right Arrow: Extend the existing folder in the left-hand panel. If the main folder is already extended, this shortcut picks the first subdirectory in it.

- Shrink the present folder using the Left arrow. If the mother folder has already been collapsed, this shortcut picks it.

- Go to the upper end of the current window by selecting Home.

- Last but not least, go to the base of the current window by pressing End.

Shortcuts for Taskbar

With the Windows taskbar buttons, the accompanying shortcuts make it easy to open software in specific ways or within certain conditions:

- Left-click on the program icon while holding down Ctrl and Shift: Access software as an admin from the Taskbar

- Create a second copy of a program with admin capabilities by pressing Win + Ctrl + Shift + Number key (0-9) together.

- Press Win + Number to launch programs from their taskbar icons. That is, pressing Win + 1 will launch the first application whose symbol is pinned to the Taskbar, while pressing Win + 2 will launch the second application, and so on, based on their Taskbar placement.

- Press Win + T to cycle between the taskbar's applications.

- From your PC's taskbar, press Win + Alt + D to see the time and date.

- Shift + Left Click app symbol: From the taskbar, launch a new copy of an application.

- Hold down Shift and right-click the clustered application icon: From the taskbar, open the session bar for the grouped applications.

- Press Win + B to select the overflow button (The Up) within the Notification Area (When selected, hit Enter and utilize directional keys to switch between the icons in the overflow list)

- Press the number keys (0-9) while holding down the Alt key. Access the Jump List for a Taskbar icon.

- Launch another copy of an active application using Win + Shift + Number Keys (0-9)

- Change to the last open window of a hooked program by pressing Win + Ctrl + Number key (0-9)

Shortcuts for Accessibility

Accessibility capabilities in Windows 11 are activated and used with the accompanying keyboard shortcuts:

- Press Win + U to access Windows Settings "Ease of Access" Center.
- Zoom and Magnifier are turned on with Win + plus (+).
- Win + minus: This will zoom out a page
- Win + Esc: Quits Magnifier
- Change to Magnifier's docked view by pressing Alt + Ctrl + D.
- Change to a complete-screen mode in the Magnifier by pressing Alt + Ctrl + F.
- Change to the lens mode in the Magnifier by pressing Alt + Ctrl + L.
- Reverse colors in the Magnifier by pressing Alt + Ctrl + I.
- Press Alt + Ctrl + M to cycle between Magnifier's perspectives.
- In Magnifier, press Alt + Ctrl + R to adjust the lens using your mouse.
- Alt + Ctrl + Arrow keys Will pan in the Magnifier
- Zoom out or in with Ctrl + Alt + mouse scroll

- Win + Enter will launch the Narrator

- In Windows 11, press Win + Ctrl + O to bring up the on-screen keyboard.

- Keep Right Shift pressed for 8 seconds: Filter Keys can be turned off and on.

- Left Alt + Left Shift + PrtSc: Enable or disable High Contrast.

- Mouse Keys On/Off: Left Alt + Left Shift + Num Lock

- Hold down Shift for five seconds: Turn off or on Sticky Keys.

- Hold down the Num Lock key for five seconds: Toggle the Toggle Keys on/off switch.

Shortcuts for the Windows Game Bar

The Windows Game Bar, which was first featured in Windows 10, provides various specific shortcut keys for ease and simplicity of usage.

- Press Win + G to access the game bar.

- Press Win + Alt + G to document the latest thirty seconds of gameplay.

- Stop or start recording a current game by pressing Win + Alt + R.

- Press Win + Alt + PrtScn to capture a snapshot of the currently playing game.

- Press Win + Alt + T to see or conceal the present game's recording timer.

Miscellaneous Shortcuts

Besides the ones mentioned in the previous section, Windows 11 comes with a slew of some other shortcuts, none of which fit neatly into any of the categories. They are as follows:

- Initiate IME reconversion by pressing Win + forward slash.

- Press Win + F to access the Feedback Hub.

- Press Win + K to access the quick setting "Connect."

- Press Win + O to lock the device's direction.

- Press Win + Pause to open Windows Settings and go to System Properties.

- Search for computers with Win + Ctrl + F

- Move a Window or application from one screen to another by pressing the Win + Shift + Right/Left arrow button.

- Press Win + Spacebar to change the input language and keyboard layout.

- Press Win + V to access the clipboard history

- Press Win + Y to swap between Windows Mixed Reality and desktop input.

- Press Win + C to open Cortana

Use the Best Windows 11 Keyboard Shortcuts

You should utilize the ideal hotkeys on Windows 11 as you've been informed about them in order to enjoy the best of Microsoft's new OS. Almost all the shortcuts function on Windows 10 and earlier editions too, so they'll become useful even when you haven't upgraded to Windows 11.

In the meantime, if you're using Windows 11 but don't like the changes, here's how to downgrade your computer from Windows 11 to Windows 10. If you're trapped with Windows 10, though, see how to obtain Windows 11 capabilities in Windows 10 as soon as. Lastly, since you're willing to take part in using hotkeys to increase your productivity, gain knowledge on how you can wipe your browsing history in Edge, Firefox, and Chrome with hotkeys.

How to Save all Necessary Information in The Browser?

Vital information can often be stored on different parts of your machine – and your browser is one of them. Like document editors, you can save vital information on your browser simply by clicking CTRL + S.

How to Change Downloads folder with Windows 11

As previously stated, the Downloads location in Windows 11 may be moved or changed to any area, including the Desktop.

To do so, follow the procedures outlined below.

- The Move command in the context menu properties of the Download folder is the simplest method to alter the standard download destination in Windows 11.
- To begin, go to the taskbar at the base of your display and select File Explorer.
- When the File Explorer window appears, right-click or press and hold on to the Downloads to bring up the Properties option.
- Choose the Location option, then the Move option once the Properties window appears.
- Then, using File Explorer, browse to the Downloads folder you created on your Desktop and select it, then choose Select Folder.

- Choose OK as soon as you've decided on a place. A window comparable to the one below will appear, requesting if you'd like to transfer all of your files to new a location from an old one.
- To make the modifications, choose Yes.
- Any item you get online after that'll be immediately stored in your Desktop's Downloads folder.

title

I would be incredibly thankful if you could take just 60 seconds to write a brief review on Amazon, even if it's just a few sentences!

>>Click here to leave a review

Conclusion

What Are the Benefits of Windows 11?

All things computerized have a paralyzing terror in the minds of older individuals. Unlike today's youngsters, they presumably only had a TV to handle during their childhoods. It's only normal for them if they are sentimental and avoid technology. However, if you're reading this, you already know how important it is to master fundamental computer skills. Use these three arguments to persuade your parents or older relatives on why they should learn how to use one:

To Handle Day-to-Day Needs

Digitization is gradually infiltrating our daily lives. Electronic repositories now house our health records. Online banking services have moved our money to the internet as well. Some activities are now far more straightforward to conduct online than offline. For a time, we can dodge these adjustments, but never forever. Take a peek around today's shops. There are fewer retail workers and more automated kiosks, albeit not all of the latter can handle cash. Seniors must learn to work with these screens regularly. With the widespread use of smartphones and the growth of banking applications such as, this might not be long before cash is phased out.

For Entertainment

If they struggle to admit they have "no option," attempt to persuade them that it is indeed a "good decision." As your folks get older, they're more likely to be working less and spend more time doing things they enjoy. Consider this: What do they enjoy doing? Do you enjoy Taiwanese dramas? Do you like listening to music from the 1970s? Do you like to read books on world politics? Whatever their hobbies, there are sure to be a plethora of applications that may immediately enhance the qualities of their living.

To Strengthen Family Ties

Older individuals are prone to want intergenerational connection in addition to entertainment. Asking for your assistance could be your older folks' method of expressing their worry! Learning fundamental PC and smartphone skills, on the other hand, will only help your parents to have more regular and good contact. Knowing how to use social media platforms is one of the most beneficial for this reason.

Seventy-seven percent of Singaporeans have access to social media platforms. Instagram isn't only for the youngsters; thirty-three percent of web users are aged between fifty-five and sixty-five. Seniors who can traverse these platforms alone will be far better able to keep up with what their kids and grandkids are doing, even if they're staying in the same house.

New Features

This section summarizes what's new in Windows 11, along with some features and enhancements.

Scanning and Security

Windows 11 has comparable privacy and security features as Windows 10. The safety of your gadgets begins with the hardware and extends to the operating system, apps, and identity, and user security. The Windows operating system has tools that can assist you in these domains. Some of these characteristics are described in this section.

- The Windows Security program is included with the operating system. This software has a user-friendly design and includes some regularly used security systems. You'll receive account protection, firewall, and network protection, virus and threat protection, and lots more.

- Security baselines are pre-configured security configurations that apply to your machines. If you lack an idea of where to begin or if you think that going through all of the configurations is too time-intensive, you want to check out the Security Baselines.

- Microsoft Defender Antivirus is an in-built security feature in Windows that helps safeguard computers with first-rate protection. Your company will benefit from robust endpoint security as well as enhanced endpoint response and protection when Microsoft Defender for Endpoint is deployed. You may establish rules depending on danger levels identified in Microsoft Defender for Endpoint if your gadgets are controlled using Endpoint Manager.

- Identities and users are protected using Windows Hello for Business. It does away with passwords and instead relies on biometric or a PIN that is stored locally on the computer. More secure hardware capabilities, like TPM chips and IR cameras, are being included by gadget makers. These capabilities work in conjunction with Windows Hello for Business where it helps safeguard user identities on office computers.

- Going password-less as an administrator aid in the security of user identities. The Windows OS, Azure AD, and Endpoint

Manager work together to ensure adherence by removing passwords, creating more robust regulations, and removing passwords. Accessibility to new services and those you are already using is made easier.

- Windows 365 is a cloud-based OS for desktop computers. You may run Windows 365 as a virtual computer from any internet-connected gadget, such as macOS systems and Android.

- Microsoft Teams is built into the operating system and appears on the taskbar by default. Users may initiate a call by selecting the chat symbol, logging in with their Microsoft account, and selecting the chat symbol.

Microsoft Teams is only available for individual accounts in this edition. You can use MDM policies like Endpoint Manager to launch the Microsoft Teams application to enterprise accounts like **user@contoso.com**.

Preinstalled applications may be managed through the **Settings app > Apps > Apps & Features** path. Admins can implement policies that pin programs to the Taskbar or disable the preset pinned applications.

- The operating system comes with **Power Automate**, a software that is designed for desktops. This low-code software allows your system users to design workflows, which provides them with some assistance for their daily activities. Users may, for instance, build workflows that save a note to OneNote, alert a workgroup whenever a new Forms answer is received, and get notifications if a member of the workgroup adds a file to the SharePoint.

- Preinstalled applications may be managed by going through this path **Settings app > Apps > Apps & Features**.

Personalize Your Desktop Experience

Snap Groups, Snap Layouts: Drag your cursor over the maximize/minimize buttons when you launch an application. You may then choose a new layout for the application:

System users could change the size of applications on their screens with this functionality. The snapped design also remains in place when you load other applications to the design.

When you save a Snap Layout with your applications, it becomes a part of the Snap Group. When you mouse across an application in an established snap layout on the taskbar, it displays all of the applications in that particular layout. Snap Group is the name of this functionality. You may choose a group, and all of the applications will launch in much the same way. You may like to toggle between Snap Groups as you introduce more by choosing the Snap Group.

The **Settings App > System > Multitasking** path can be used to control various snap capabilities. Snap Layouts may also be added to apps that your company produces.

Start Menu

By default, certain programs are set to the Start menu. You may change the appearance of the Start menu by unpinning (and pinning) the applications you desire. You may, for instance, pin frequently used applications in your company, like Microsoft Teams, Outlook, applications your company develops, and lots more.

You may use policy to distribute your unique Start menu appearance to your company's computers.

The **Settings App > Personalization** path allows users to customize various aspects of the Start menu.

Taskbar

The Taskbar allows users to unpin (and pin) applications. You may, for instance, pin frequently used applications in your company, like

Microsoft Teams, Outlook, applications your company produces, and more. You may launch your personalized Taskbar to computers in your company via policy.

The **Settings App > Personalization** path allows users to customize various Taskbar functions.

Taskbar Widgets

Widgets can be found on the Taskbar. It has a customized feed with calendar, weather, news, stock prices, and some other information:

You may disable\enable this function with the Computer Administrative\ConfigurationWindows\TemplatesWidgets\Components Group Policy.

Also, you can create a custom Taskbar for your company's machines.

Virtual Desktops

To create new desktops, click the Desktops symbol on the Taskbar. Contingent on what you are working on, you can employ the desktop to launch different programs. You may, for instance, build a Travel desktop that comprises travel-related applications and websites.

You may like to launch a personalized Taskbar to computers in your workplace via policy.

The **Settings App > System > Multitasking** path allows you to control various desktop functions. Improved versions of your existing programs

All of your Windows 10 applications will by default run on Windows 11. If there are any problems, the App Assure can come in handy.

For your Win32, UWP, WInForm, and WPF desktop app files, you may keep using the MSIX files. To deploy Windows applications, keep using Windows Package Manager. To virtualize applications and desktops, employ the Azure Virtual Desktop with the MSIX application attachment.

System users can adjust various app configurations via the Settings app > Apps route. They can download programs from wherever, but they'll alert the user if there is a similar application in the Microsoft Store. They may also select which applications launch when they log in.

You may build policies that govern some application data with an MDM provider such as Endpoint Manager.

If you use Endpoint Manager in managing your devices, you're probably already acquainted with the Company Portal software. The Company Portal, which debuted with Windows 11, is a private application hub for your organization's applications. Keep using the Microsoft Store for retail and public applications.

Device Compatibility

After Microsoft revealed its first significant OS upgrade in six years on October 4th, the main concern on many computer users' minds has been: will my device be compliant? Following Microsoft's major disclosure of the upgraded operating system, there has been some uncertainty over device interoperability. The simple answer, as per a corporate blog post, is that Windows 11 should operate with most computers. Even though its release date finally arrived, Microsoft warns you should wait till mid-2022 to profitably use Windows 11.

Unfortunately, when Microsoft initially officially confirmed Windows 11 in the dawn of 2021, its software for establishing interoperability, the PC Health Check tool, didn't give users sufficient details about why their machines weren't compliant, so Microsoft temporarily suspended the application. Microsoft's PC Health Check, on the other hand, is currently up and running. The program will inform you if your machine satisfies the Windows 11 system requirements, and if it does not, it'll explain why and give connections to more resources.

However, this isn't the only option to see if your computer is compatible with the Windows 11 upgrade. Continue reading to learn about all of your choices for determining whether or not your device is compatible with Windows 11. It's important to verify if your PC is compliant with Windows 11. If your computer does not match the qualifying standards, you might have to upgrade it by 2025, since Microsoft will be phased out of Windows 10 in the following few years.

Check your computer's compatibility with Windows 11 using Microsoft's PC Health Check software.

To see if your PC matches the system requirements for Windows 11, follow these instructions.

1. Get the **PC Health Check** from Microsoft. Install after opening the file and agreeing to the user agreement. Ensure the box labeled **"Open PC Health Check"** is selected, then hit **Finish**.

2. The application home page that appears reads, **"PC health at a glance."** **"Introducing Windows 11,"** reads a box at the top. Select **Check**. If your computer isn't compliant, you'll receive a notice that reads "This PC does not presently meet Windows 11 requirements."

You can get the Windows 11 upgrade for no cost if your system is eligible.

Microsoft has planned a phased deployment, with many machines not receiving the update until 2022.

To see if Windows 11 is compatible, use the WhyNotWin11 program. WhyNotWin11, an open-source program, is a decent option for the PC Health Check application. The Github application, which was built by a non-Microsoft developer, has a somewhat less user-friendly design, but it should provide you with greater details and go into greater depth about different potential compliance concerns.

Browse through Microsoft's overview of Windows 11 system requirements.

To see if your computer is compliant with Windows 11, go to Microsoft's website and look at the overview of system requirements. You may get the Windows 11 upgrade for nothing if your system is suitable.

What Are the Benefits of Windows 11?

All things computerized have a paralyzing terror in the minds of older individuals. Unlike today's youngsters, they presumably only had a TV to handle during their childhoods. It's only normal for them if they are sentimental and avoid technology. However, if you're reading this, you already know how important it is to master fundamental computer skills. Use these three arguments to persuade your parents or older relatives on why they should learn how to use one:

Handling Day-to-Day Needs

Digitization is gradually infiltrating our daily lives. Electronic repositories now house our health records. Online banking services have moved our money to the internet as well. Some activities are now far more straightforward to conduct online than offline. For a time, we can dodge these adjustments, but never forever. Take a peek around today's shops. There are fewer retail workers and more automated kiosks, albeit not all of the latter can handle cash. Seniors must learn to work with these screens regularly. With the widespread use of smartphones and the growth of banking applications, this might not be long before cash is phased out.

Entertainment

If they struggle to admit they have "no option," attempt to persuade them that it is indeed a "good decision." As your folks get older, they're more likely to be working less and spend more time doing things they enjoy. Consider this: What do they enjoy doing? Do you enjoy Taiwanese dramas? Do you like listening to music from the 1970s? Do you like to read books on world politics? Whatever their hobbies, there are sure to be a plethora of applications that may immediately enhance the qualities of their living.

To Strengthen Family Ties

Older individuals are prone to want intergenerational connection in addition to entertainment. Asking for your assistance could be your older folks' method of expressing their worry! Learning fundamental PC and smartphone skills, on the other hand, will only help your parents to have more regular and good contact. Knowing how to use social media platforms is one of the most beneficial for this reason. Seventy-seven percent of Singaporeans have access to social media platforms. Instagram isn't only for the youngsters; thirty-three percent of web users are aged between fifty-five and sixty-five. Seniors who can traverse these platforms alone will be far better able to keep up with what their kids and grandkids are doing, even if they're staying in the same house.

The coming of the latest Windows in the Windows community was indeed a joyous one. Most Windows fans can now work in a more productive and interesting environment. While it satisfied the bulk of Windows users, the new Windows 11 was somewhat uninteresting to some other users. The elimination of some applications and functionalities and the redesign wasn't something they were particularly interested in. Windows 11 cuts through complexity and helps you focus on what's important.

But some other notable inclusion made up for this elimination. For instance, the new Microsoft Store brings together your favorite apps and entertainment. What more? Windows 11 is faster, safer, and more familiar for IT professionals. Now is the time to buy a Window 11-powered PC!

Printed in Great Britain
by Amazon